D1273216

I Lost It At The Video Store

I Lost It At The Video Store

A Filmmakers' Oral History of a Vanished Era

Tom Roston

The Critical Press
Raleigh, NC

Publisher's Cataloging-in-Publication Data

Roston, Tom

I lost it at the video store: a filmmakers' oral history of a vanished era / Tom Roston.

pages cm

LCCN 2015941789

ISBN 978-1-941629-15-4 (hardcover)

ISBN 978-1-941629-17-8 (electronic book text)

1. Film 2. History & Criticism

Cover Designed by Alex Kittle.

"Passing of a Video Store and a Downtown Aesthetic" originally published by *The New York Times,* July 24th, 2014.

Contents

Introduction: Strangers in Paradise

Jean-Luc Godard's *Contempt* flickered from the television that hung from the ceiling. In fact, the same film was on during three separate visits to Kim's Video in Manhattan's East Village. Each time, the 1963 French New Wave lament over personal estrangement and the tension between art and commerce played with the sound turned off. And also, each time, it was accompanied by different music on the sound system. First, there was R&B, then a Yemeni oud arrangement, and finally a low, ambient, engine-room sound reminiscent of the *Eraserhead* soundtrack.

The first combination was ironic and playful; the

second, exotic and political; the third, ominous and despairing. The different juxtapositions between sound and image made each experience a distinct, cerebral and transportive reminder of what great video stores used to be: shrines to cinema, but also subversions, and always on their own terms.

I was writing a story for *The New York Times* about the closing of Kim's during the summer of 2014, and I focused on the changing of the downtown cultural landscape. I spoke with artists and other creative types who had frequented Kim's.

The last incarnation of Kim's Video closed in the summer of 2014.

"Everything in my life, I can somehow attribute to finding Kim's," chef and author Eddie Huang said. The change of the cultural sensibility was, I thought, best personified by Richard Hell, the punk musician who was once an inspiration for the Sex Pistols, and later a Kim's regular. Back in the day, Hell used to live in the filth and ghostwrite papers for students from Andrew Sarris' Hitchcock classes at Columbia for seventy-five dollars apiece. I met Hell at the store, while the Kim's clerks talked about the merits of *True Romance*. Hell looked for the *Contempt* DVD before deciding it wasn't worth spending thirty bucks on it, anyway. We left to conduct our interview.

Before reporting that article, I hadn't been to Kim's in almost a decade. In fact, I hadn't been inside any video store in that same period of time. I'm not including the sterile, plastic-wrapped aisles at Best Buy or Wal-Mart I'd passed by over the years. For home viewing, I had given in to the conveniences of industry screeners, Netflix, occasional iTunes downloads, and the scraps I could find on television.

Overnight, it seems, the video store disappeared from most of our lives. It left as quickly as it appeared. The VCR and Betamax tapes were introduced as high-priced curios in 1976. Video rental stores were spreading across the land by 1980. And, suddenly, the trip to the video store became an integral part of our everyday lives throughout the 1980s and 1990s. Home viewing entered a new phase with the introduction of DVDs in 1997. It kept growing until the early 2000s when there were more than thirty thousand video stores (a number that includes gas stations, convenience stores and other outlets) in the country.

But the decline was rapid and unsparing. The industry collapsed in the five years since DVDs peaked in 2004. Blockbuster, which began with one store in 1985, had also peaked in 2004, but it declared bankruptcy in 2010. The chain store had already gutted the mom-and-pop video industry.

True, video stores still exist. At the end of 2014, in addition to mom-and-pop stragglers, there are a couple dozen independent Blockbusters that retain the name. And there is Family Video, a midwestern chain that claims more than seven hundred stores. And there are still some great ones, like Scarecrow in Seattle, Vidiots and CineFile in Los Angeles, Le Video in San Francisco, Facets in Chicago, and Video Free Brooklyn. But those could disappear any day—Vidiots was about to close its doors in 2014 until Megan Ellison's Annapurna Pictures swooped in to save it for now—and the video store has become a faint projection of what it once was, an anachronism lurking in the looming shadow of the Internet.

Having already begun work on this book before going to Kim's for the *Times*, I'd given all of this plenty of thought, but that didn't prepare me for the physical experience. As I walked into the store while Brigitte Bardot and Michel Piccoli badgered each other mutely overhead, I was gripped by a visceral memory of being sixteen and entering the video store—not that one, but the many I frequented between the ages of fifteen and thirty—and standing in the aisles of shelves with sections designated by director, cult, foreign, comedy, sci-fi, new releases, girls with guns, time travel, and what have you.

The Kim's I wrote about was just a shell of its former self. It was the last outpost after Mr. Kim had closed each of his stores, including the three-story movie geek mecca on St. Mark's. "I am the loser," Mr. Kim said, grimly. "Netflix is the winner."

Still, being there brought me back to the stores during their glory years, when I was a teen, my whole life ahead of me. I got a flash of what I didn't know then, that the innervating thrill I was feeling was my evolving self finding a receptive shelf in each aisle. Everything I was feeling, thinking, exploring, fighting, desiring, fleeing, was there. My fomenting identity could find an external corollary for every mood. And every corner promised a new possibility, a new way of life, a new hero I might identify with, or new girl I could fall for.

The interior of Kim's Video.

Those shelves felt limitless but also within reach. I may not have been the emerging filmmaker you'll find in this book, but I was working through some heavy angst, repeatedly watching *Pink Floyd: The Wall* and *A Clockwork Orange*, not for the aesthetic appreciation—although that would come—but because they spoke to me. Whether it was the films of Hal Hartley, Werner Herzog, or Jim Jarmusch, each director's shelf promised a particular filmmaker's vision; a private, personal mentorship.

There wasn't just one store for me. I went to the Blockbusters that were nearby on the Upper West of Manhattan, or, later, on Greenwich Avenue downtown. But I preferred independents like Kim's and

World of Video in New York City. There were others, in Providence, Rhode Island, and Washington, D.C., but the store that felt most like my own private Idaho was Just Videos in Brattleboro, Vermont, where my family spent vacations. Just Videos was a strangely shaped store, tucked in a corner of the Harmony Parking Lot. And the store's owner, artist William Hayes, curated it perfectly for my brain; it's where I explored the visions of many of my favorite directors, from the Coen brothers to Stanley Kubrick to Martin Scorsese.

Eventually, it became a part of my profession. At Kim's, I supplemented my film knowledge when I was an editor at *Premiere*, a now-defunct movie magazine.

If I had let it, the experience of returning to Kim's would have been crushing. The weight of loss—of my youth and that phase of unbridled movie fandom—would have been too much. Oh, how the shelves could talk! But it was pretty funny, too. I laughed when I noticed *Brothers McMullen* was in the comedy section, and not in the U.S. directors' section. It felt like a not-so-subtle wink from the clerks about their feelings regarding the Eddie Burns oeuvre.

That sort of unspoken, intuitive communication is the fabric of a culture. And what I hope to do with this book is show that those threads extended beyond our individual experiences to a wide swath of America that included the filmmakers themselves. As much as the video store was a part of my, and possibly your, coming-of-age story, it was even more so for them. They dedicated their lives to what they saw in those aisles. Their films are a product of video store culture, both creatively and financially, as you'll see in these pages.

And who better than the filmmakers, who rode the wave of the emergence of the video store, to tell its story? Not only are they great storytellers, but they are also the direct beneficiaries of the film-gorging open season that the video store wrought, so that they could talk their way inside and out of a Bergman or Polanski flick.

This wouldn't have worked hadn't these guys been so smart and self-aware about it. (I want to note, however, that it's unfortunate that they're mostly white guys gathered here.) My first interview for the book was with Tim Blake Nelson, an actor (*O Brother, Where Art Thou?*) and director (*The Grey Zone*) I've known for many years, and who quickly convinced me that I was on the right path.

"What video stores and the proliferation of videos did was to democratize access to movies and to film history," Nelson said, while taking a break from working on the sound editing for his fifth directorial effort, *Anesthesia*. "You used to have to take a class or luck into the odd Sunday afternoon movie or late-night movie special to get a sense of film history. And even then, there were portions excised and commercial interruptions. This had a really big impact on emerging filmmakers who understood the subjectivity of movies, because they could much more easily juxtapose a Hitchcock film with a Scorsese film, with films by David Lean, John Ford, or John Huston, and then with a Tobe Hooper movie, which is what we all did."

Nelson and I have had a connection perhaps burnished by sharing an alma mater, Brown University (although not concurrently), and I have been deeply grateful to him for being such a great source. Partly bred by our school years, we, like most of the filmmakers in this book, share a pleasure at thinking about the films we love critically. That, too, was something bred in the video store, "the great equalizer," as director J.C. Chandor said.

Consider this, also from Nelson:

"By learning to convert movies to a videotape and then watching them on a TV screen, there is a natural progression to off-line editing, where you are editing on a screen with digitized images. And this, I will always aver, changed how we make movies. That's in the proliferation of close-ups in movies now. Since the advent of the video, most films are seen on small screens, and so the wide shot, or what Scorsese would call "the shot," a real composition that is not just about somebody's face, no longer prevails as a part of the film aesthetic. We're so eager to get in there and see a face because we are seeing movies on the same screens on which we're editing movies, and we don't trust the figure being small in the frame. Whereas, when the movie theater was the sole venue in which you were going to see a movie, the wide shot with a figure in the foreground or in the background was just giving you a lot more visual information. I have to resist the impulse to dispense with wide shots when wide shots are very beautiful and, more importantly, they're often quite philosophical."

I include this quote partly because it's a perceptive mouthful that's emblematic of how some of these filmmakers think, but also because it demonstrates the parameters of this book. It's not going to get more technical than that. This history is primarily a story. It's a narrative about the relationship between the filmmakers and the video store.

I could use a broader brush and talk more about how the video store was one of the last vestiges of media's analog world—and you'll hear some of that toward the end—but this is essentially a filmmakers' collective memoir that embodies a theory: that the video store, both financially and formally, was an irreplaceable part of the independent film movement of the 1980s and 1990s.

Before I take a bow, let me introduce you to producer and indie film pioneer John Pierson, who had this to say about my thesis: "Of course it's true," Pierson said. "And it's not exactly your theory."

I appreciated Pierson's salty retort because it was both affirming and illuminating: What *is* unique about this project is that it's being told by the filmmakers. In 2013, when Blockbuster shuttered its doors, there were many requiems written by fans and journalists. But I wanted to hear from the filmmakers. So I set out to frame our individual video store experiences within that of a generation of filmmakers who came of age between 1980 and 2005.

If you are reading this book, it is likely that you, in some way, "lost it" at the video store, just as they did. Or perhaps, young grasshopper, you just wish you had. Either way, I hope you'll enjoy the rewind.

I can't deny getting a knot in my throat when I recall the video jacket that riveted me most; Herzog's *Aguirre, Wrath of God*, with its image of actor Klaus Kinski in that ridiculous helmet and eyes blazing. It was edifying to hear that jacket had a similar impression on James Franco. And also Darren Aronofsky; so much so that he now has the poster hanging on a wall in his office.

There I go, getting sentimental again. So let's steer this back to the evolution of film and grounded in the financial foundation on which the video store stands. Cue director Joe Swanberg for his big-picture take:

"My honest opinion is that this is the evolution of a marketing machine. In the 1930s, when a movie finished its run, they threw it in the garbage. The product expired in the same way bad milk expired. They burned the negative. It was taking up space in the storage room. They made the money they were going to make. No one wanted to house them. In the eighties, it was like, 'Holy shit! People really still want to watch *Gone with the Wind*. And they also kind of want to own *Gone with the Wind*.' They were like, 'Cool. We already made *Gone with the Wind*. Now, we can make an additional twenty bucks a pop.' I don't see the eighties video revolution being created by cinephiles, who were saying, 'We have to give people access to the movies.' It was studio number crunching. And they were like, 'Oh yeah, this makes total sense.'"

True, but a profit motive behind the emergence of home video doesn't negate its democratizing and film–fanatic–friendly impact. How it played out isn't something you can only find on a profit/loss spreadsheet; you also have to take into account lives expanded, minds inspired, and careers progressed.

And we will get to that in all its glory. But I think it would be helpful if I first give a quick synopsis of how the video store came to be. I put this together primarily by using several sources, including my interviews and Daniel Herbert's fine book, *Videoland: Movie Culture at the American Video Store*.

In the Beginning . . .

Movies were once intended to be seen in movie theaters. Although some early 20th-century homes were equipped with 16-millimeter projectors for home movie viewing, they were far and few between. After television sets became a standard living room fixture in the mid-1950s, they began airing movies. In the early 1960s, NBC began with the primetime series, "Saturday Night at the Movies." Other networks soon followed.

PBS programmed a show, "Film Odyssey," hosted by Charles Champlin, which featured well-curated films, such as *8½*, *Jules and Jim*, *Knife in the Water*, and *Seven Samurai*, along with interviews with the directors. "It was mind-blowing," said John Pierson, who, like millions of other budding film lovers, including his future wife, Janet, "got turned on to art films" through the 1972 series.

There were also repertory theaters, where classic and foreign films were exhibited. New York City's Film Forum, which had opened in 1970, was a leader of a thriving national repertory scene that lasted well into the 1980s. Film Forum helped restore films such as *Once Upon a Time in the West* and *400 Blows*.

And film societies were prevalent, mainly on university campuses. Studios didn't want anyone else to own their movie prints, so they would lease their films out to the societies for a period of time. Those organizations would then host movie nights for their respective audiences.

Although the ability to record video images had been in development in Japan since the 1950s, the first VCRs entered the market in the mid-1970s. Sony had its better-image quality Betamax tape, while other companies, including JVC and Matsushita, were working on a VHS tape that was larger, but could provide more recording and playing time. VHS-playing VCRs were introduced in 1977, and the first video store opened later that year.

Andre Blay, who had been making corporate training films through his company Magnetic Video, negotiated the first licensing deal with a studio, 20th Century Fox, so that he could get access to fifty of its titles, including *Tora! Tora! Tora!*, *Patton*, *The French Connection*, *The Sound of Music*, and *Butch Cassidy and the Sundance Kid*. Blay sold his tapes to electronics stores, as well as to consumers directly through a mail-order company, Video Club of America. Concerned about his profit margins, he asked retailers to sign agreements that they would not rent the videos to consumers. That didn't stop a flourishing rental business.

At first, VCRs were a high-priced item, costing more than $1,000. Nevertheless, video stores started to pop up in neighborhoods. "In 1979 or 1980, you would be going to a place where someone had turned a jewelry store into a video store and the cases were still there, but instead of diamonds, they had boxes of these movies," says Larry Estes, who went from running the film program at the University of Georgia to being a home video executive in New York City and then in Los Angeles. "You'd notice that there were these Fox films on one side, and the rest of the store was porn because the pornography business shortcut the need to go through all the licensing. It was kind of freaky. Two-thirds of the store was literally porn."

The studios had been initially skeptical of the new technology, concerned that it was going to blow a hole in its business model of people watching movies in theaters. And they were worried that people would tape movies playing on television, especially on emerging cable channels like HBO, and then pass them on to friends. They were right. Another major force diminishing the studio returns was that video stores were primarily renting out their copyrighted material for multiple viewings. And so the studios joined together to litigate against the rental industry.

Ultimately, they lost under what's known as the first-sale doctrine. Ira Deutchman, a movie executive and Columbia professor, explained the concept as similar to when a collector buys a Picasso painting from Picasso. If the collector then turns around and sells the painting for a profit, he is not obligated to pass any gains back to Picasso. The Supreme Court decision protected video stores as long as they didn't make copies of the copyrighted material.

As the case made its way through the courts, the rental business was booming, albeit in fits and starts. "In its formative stages in the early 1980s, some people thought it was going to be a big deal and some didn't," Estes says. "Generally, people at the studios thought it was lark, a souvenir, fun thing, like merchandising."

That pretty much brings us up to speed to when this oral history begins. Swanberg is right in asserting that home video was fundamentally an innovation to sell a product, but what's more relevant here is that the evolution of the video store provided gaps and crevices and, yes, shelf space, where original, nimble filmmakers could get a foothold.

Moneymaking interests and artistic inclinations

aligned. Where studios were slow, independents—from distributors to directors—were quick to take advantage of the fertile, if sometimes fetid, soil.

"It's always, 'Who needs product? Who needs this? How can I provide it so I can get the money to make it?'" says director Allison Anders. "That's where the filmmakers go."

Anders, who was in film school at UCLA in the early 1980s, recalls a teaching assistant announcing that students needed to take notes during class screenings because they'd need to refer to them when writing papers. And then he added wistfully, "Maybe somewhere in the future, we'll all have personal video machines in our houses so we can refer back and rewatch things."

It seemed, even then, "preposterous," she says. The video revolution was well under way, but it hadn't reached one of the nation's leading film schools. And then suddenly it was upon us.

Although it's tempting to mark 1977, the introduction of the VHS-playing VCR, and 2013, the year that Blockbuster closed its doors, as the beginning and ending of the video store era, I would propose 1980 to 2005 as the beginning and end, because those years more closely match the actual entrance and exit of the video store as a dominant force on the cultural landscape.

That also syncs with a birth generation, which is approximately twenty-five years. That would put Generation X, people born roughly between 1963 and 1980, as most squarely coming of age during the video store era. Of course, none of these numbers are fixed. There were late bloomers and early adopters and different ways that different filmmakers were affected by the video store.

For instance, I would position John Sayles, born in 1950, as a part of the video store revolution because his influence and his films took root there. I'd do the same with Herzog, born in 1942, whose early films (*Aguirre, Fitzcarraldo, Nosferatu, The Vampyre*) once sparkled so bewitchingly from the shelves. But he wouldn't.

In reply to my interview request, Herzog politely declined, noting that he had "not participated in the video store culture," he wrote in an email. "In fact, I have never rented a video or a DVD, and I only remember having set my foot in one of the stores one single time in my life in order to sign DVDs of my own films."

So, yes, the video store era is built on somewhat fluid designations. There is a video store filmmaker identity that has become codified in the popular imagination, best exemplified by directors Quentin Tarantino and Kevin Smith, along with their first films, *Reservoir Dogs* and *Clerks*. And a straight line sure can be drawn from Tarantino and Smith (born, respectively, in 1963 and 1970) to younger clerk filmmakers Swanberg and Alex Ross Perry (born 1981 and 1984). These two sets of filmmakers hue closest to providing the generational bookends to the video store era.

But the other voices here indicate that there was a varied influence that extended beyond any particular generation or gender or whether one worked as a clerk at a store.

Does this oral history include every filmmaker associated with the video store? Unfortunately, no. But I hope you'll agree that it achieves the quorum necessary to give the era its true shape.

You may notice that some of the voices contradict each other. That's intentional. I wanted this to flow like a conversation. And I arranged the chapters thematically to cover the many influences (personal, creative, financial) that defined the relationship between the filmmakers and the video store.

And you should be aware of my editing process—outside of John and Janet Pierson, none of these interviews were conducted together—so this is a reanimated monster of my own creation. To the best of my ability, I was faithful to what each of my generous interview subjects said and what I thought they intended. You may also want to know that, although there's plenty of adult language (and content, actually; thanks to the red-band ravings of Mr. Smith), I cut a number of F-bombs, not to be puritanical, but because cussing can sometimes detract from what someone's saying.

We are in a period of transition when it comes to how movies are distributed and exhibited in theaters and to our homes. As I write these words, I await the delivery of a new flat-screen television that will finally replace my boxy, decade-old set. I've been holding out partly because I dread the "soap opera effect." I am wary of the way movies are going to look in this new, but not necessarily better, digital age. I hear the smart TV options aren't so smart. Still, I am moving forward.

Streaming is fraught with frustration. But there is promise. You'll see both sides of that spectrum expressed in the later chapters.

But while the future is unclear, the dust has finally settled on the video store. Holdouts still exist, and I hope they find a way to keep the lights on, even if they become museums. (David O. Russell and others believe they should be regarded as institutions for cultural preservation). But their cultural and financial reign is over.

"When the end of the story is in sight, it's easier to

see the arc," Deutchman says. "There is an historical perspective that didn't exist even eight or nine years ago."

In 2015, as more and more stores disappear, the dwindling DVD rental market is dominated by Redbox's automated kiosks. There are more than forty thousand of the vending machines (which, aiyee, were originally a McDonald's venture) across the country. Yes, the Criterion Collection remains an invaluable outpost for film aficionado home viewing. But Best Buy and Wal-Mart are where most people now go to buy DVDs. I think it's safe to say that film-makers will never want to eulogize these latter-day home-viewing venues.

During the interviews for this book, I often thought of my Proustian moment at Kim's. I, too, smelled the distinct smells of the moldy store that Darren Aronofsky recalled. I also felt the repulsion-attraction toward the insouciant young clerks described by Kevin Smith. And I was struck with the covetous instinct to possess films in their shiny, plastic cases just as Nicole Holofcener fondly remembered.

But when I was younger, all I was thinking about was what the movies could do for me. I didn't consider how I was a part of a greater, symphonic arrangement between fans, filmmakers, and films. Now, I know.

With her exquisite and rhapsodic reviews, which were first collected in the book, *I Lost it at the Movies*, critic Pauline Kael helped define the ardor between the audience, directors, and cinema. The title of this book is a nod to her, and a reminder that what ultimately unites the voices here is a passion for film that, for a short period of time, went for a wild ride down the aisles.

Filmmaker Glossary

(Select Film and Television Credits)

Allison Anders—Director: *Gas, Food, Lodging* (1992), *Grace of My Heart* (1996), *Orange Is the New Black* (2014).

Darren Aronofsky—Director: *Pi* (1998), *Black Swan* (2010), *Noah* (2014).

Luc Besson—Director: *Subway* (1985), *La Femme Nikita* (1990), *Lucy* (2014).

J.C. Chandor—Director: *Margin Call* (2011), *All Is Lost* (2013), *A Most Violent Year* (2014).

Ira Deutchman—Producer/Distribution Executive;

Cinecom, Fine Line Films, Emerging Pictres. *The Brother from Another Planet* (1984), *My Own Private Idaho* (1991), *Hoop Dreams* (1994).

Tom DiCillo—Director: *Johnny Suede* (1991), *Living in Oblivion* (1995), *Chicago Fire* (2014).

Larry Estes—Producer/Home Entertainment Executive; Columbia/RCA. *Sex, Lies, and Videotape* (1989), *Gas, Food, Lodging* (1992), *One False Move* (1992)

James Franco—Actor/Director: *Spider-Man* (2002), *127 Hours* (2010), *The Sound and the Fury* (2014).

Richard Gladstein—Producer/Home Entertainment Executive; LIVE Entertainment, Miramax, Film-Colony. *Silent Night, Deadly Night 3* (1989), *Reservoir Dogs* (1992), *The Hateful Eight* (2015).

Nicole Holofcener—Director: *Walking and Talking* (1996), *Lovely and Amazing* (2001), *Enough Said* (2013). Former video store clerk.

Ted Hope—Producer/Executive; Good Machine, Amazon Original Movies. *Trust* (1990), *The Brothers McMullen* (1995), *The Ice Storm* (1997).

Doug Liman—Director: *Swingers* (1996), *The Bourne Identity* (2002), *Edge of Tomorrow* (2014).

Greg Mottola—Director: *The Daytrippers* (1996), *Superbad* (2007), *The Newsroom* (2014).

Tim Blake Nelson—Actor/Director: *Eye of God* (1997), *O Brother, Where Art Thou?* (2000), *Leaves of Grass* (2009).

Alex Ross Perry—Director: *Impolex* (2009), *The Color Wheel* (2009), *Listen Up Philip* (2014).

Janet Pierson—Exhibitor/Festival Head; Film Forum, SXSW.

John Pierson—Producer/Film Representative: *She's Gotta Have It* (1986), *Slacker* (1991), *Clerks* (1994). Author of *Spike, Mike, Slackers & Dykes: A Guided Tour Across a Decade of American Independent Cinema* (1995).

David O. Russell—Director: *Spanking the Monkey* (1994), *The Fighter* (2010), *American Hustle* (2013).

John Sayles—Director: *Return of the Secaucus Seven* (1979), *The Brother from Another Planet* (1984), *Go for Sisters* (2013).

Kevin Smith—Director: *Clerks* (1994), *Chasing Amy* (1997), *Tusk* (2014). Former video store clerk.

Morgan Spurlock—Director: *Super Size Me* (2004), *The Greatest Movie Ever Sold* (2011), *One Direction: This is Us* (2013).

Joe Swanberg—Director: *Kissing on the Mouth* (2005), *Hannah Takes the Stairs* (2007), *Drinking Buddies* (2013). Former video store clerk.

Quentin Tarantino—Director: *Reservoir Dogs* (1992), *Pulp Fiction* (1994), *The Hateful Eight* (2015). Former video store clerk.

Losing It

"Everywhere you reached, there was goodness."

Kevin Smith: The first time I saw a VHS tape was at this dude's house, who worked at the post office with my father. It was 1982. He had just split up from his family, so he was living in a bachelor pad and he had this VCR. My father sold it to me by saying, "He has a machine and you can watch *Star Wars* on it."

Quentin Tarantino: Back in 1978 and 1979, when I didn't even remotely have a video player, I bought Beta copies of *Yojimbo* and *Assault on Precinct 13*. I held on to them for years. I just had the tapes. I figured, "One of these days, I'll get a VCR." Naturally, when I got a player, I didn't get a Beta.

Darren Aronofsky: I can remember the smell of the store. It always had the mildew smell of the carpet. Or maybe it was the old boxes. This was at Video on the Bay in Sheepshead Bay, in Brooklyn.

Alex Ross Perry: Five minutes down the road in suburban Philadelphia was a West Coast Video, with carpeting, and Hollywood lighting in the store. It was connected to a cookie bakery, so it always smelled like cookies.

Morgan Spurlock: My mom would drive me. This would have been the early eighties. In West Virginia. It was called Joe's Video or something like that, and it was set up in a trailer. You would rent movies out of this guy's mobile home that he turned into a video store. The videos lined the walls, and he put two rows in the middle. So basically two people couldn't stand in a row together. You could go down a row single file, and if somebody wanted to get by, you had to go around the whole row to get back to where you were.

James Franco: Midtown Video was not far from my house in Palo Alto, on the other side of town from

Stanford. It was in this little shopping area where there was a Baskin-Robbins. I loved those Friday nights we'd pick a movie. I would just go and I would browse. They would have the different areas, like horror and comedy and action. And they'd have these VHS boxes velcroed to the wall. We would never get the horror movies because we were with my mom, but I would go to the section and look at *Re-Animator*. My fourth grade teacher had said, "If you guys ever want to see a scary movie, see *Re-Animator*." I would always be drawn to boxes like that. I'd read them over and over again, and never see the movie, but they would have a place in my consciousness.

Kevin Smith: My mom says, "You can rent whatever you want." So me and my friend Mike Bellicose go up to the counter and say, "What's the sickest horror movie you have?" We're thinking *Shining*, *Friday the 13th*, *American Werewolf in London*. And he goes, "Here," and he gives us a copy of *Bloodsucking Freaks*. We sit down to watch the movie. And my mom is in the kitchen. It's very grindhouse. There are a lot of naked ladies. We didn't know that. We had asked the clerk for the sickest horror movie, and his interpretation of "sickest horror movie" was truly sick. You have to forgive me; I've never finished the movie based on what happened next. The guy who is the villain, he's holding a bunch of women prisoner. There was a line that brought my mom out of the kitchen and into the living room, slamming the stop button on the Betamax so hard that the button remained off for the entire time that we had the Betamax. My mom heard the guy go, "Her mouth will make an interesting urinal." My mom smoked into the room, and—Bam!

Morgan Spurlock: I feel like I was in the video store every other day.

Kevin Smith: Even though it was terrible, for a magic moment we were watching a movie. We were cinematic gods commanding a movie to start, playing on our command in our living room. Luckily, there was a backup flick as well.

Quentin Tarantino: For easily a decade, and even into the nineties, any time I saw a video store, and especially a mom-and-pop store, I always went to see what they had. I would go in and I would literally look at every single thing they had. I was constantly going into video stores to build up my collection, either cross taping them or buying them. Sometimes in a foreign store, I'd just steal them. I stole this Alain Delon crime film called *Big Guns*. I was just being a movie guy. I was seeking out stuff that I didn't know was out there.

Richard Gladstein: The video store was Quentin's library and his school. It was a vast collection of movies, and that's how he got to see them. You could probably credit the video store for providing the arena for him to educate himself.

Joe Swanberg: I skipped the prom to work at the video store. I was so happy to be there, I was probably watching three films a day, plus whatever we put on the TVs at work. It was a period of rabid consumption, totally building the baseline of my movie knowledge.

Quentin Tarantino: People didn't rent just one movie. They wanted what they wanted. And then they supplemented that with two others. Something oddball. Impulse buys. A Western, maybe. A classic. And they discovered all kinds of stuff. Leaving your house and going to a place where there are three thousand movies, all with enticing boxes, and hopefully with staff who are not complete idiots. And you go and you look and you shop and you see what shouts out to you, what speaks to you, what's exciting.

Nicole Holofcener: It's similar to a bookstore. When I go into a bookstore, I am so happy to be in there and to look at the spines of the books and to go around that corner and see what author will be there. And just to see what they've got. And there was the tactile nature of the whole experience.

Kevin Smith: It was the power of cinema in my hands. From 1983 to 1989, I was a video store junkie who went every day. "Can you put me on the reserve list for *Breakfast Club*?" I had just seen it, and they're like, "What's *Breakfast Club*?" Everywhere you reached, there was goodness. Even if it was *King Solomon's Mines* with Richard Chamberlain, "Fuck it. It's a movie. Pop it in." Even if the movie sucked, you were going to see four or five good trailers of movies you hadn't heard of.

An Education

"That was my IMDb: physically walking around the store and matching names."

David O. Russell: I was like, "Oh, my God. I can watch movies without going to a movie theater, I can study them—which had a massive impact on me. I got a videotape of *Chinatown*, which I watched obsessively, and then I just kept re-renting and re-renting, and they said, "Other people want it." I said, "I just really don't want to return it." I memorized a thirty-minute sequence of *Chinatown*, which is how I taught myself filmmaking.

Joe Swanberg: I read John Pierson's book, *Spike,*

Mike, Slackers, and Dykes. It was a huge, life-changing thing for me to discover that book. That book became the Bible. That book sent me to the video store with a list of a hundred films I had to see. That became my film school before I went to film school.

Janet Pierson: The way people inhaled movies once there were VCRs, you couldn't do that in the repertory days, even if you saw a lot. I'm surrounded all the time by people in their twenties and thirties who have seen everything I've seen. We lost the movie theater culture, but we gained this sort of voluminous history.

Darren Aronofsky: I remember *Pink Flamingos* being on video and someone telling me to rent it. That's how I was introduced to John Waters. Those underground films got so much more exposure because of the video store. More ideas got out there, and more underground ideas got out there quicker.

Joe Swanberg: I rented *Raising Arizona.* That was the movie that made me want to become a filmmaker. Somebody made that movie. The Coen brothers' sensibility, their sense of humor, actually made it into that movie, and that was why I liked it more than other movies. It was a light bulb moment for me: "So, not all movies are made by Steven Spielberg and star Tom Hanks. There is weird shit out there."

Richard Gladstein: I used to go into the video store and pick up a box, and look at the artwork and flip it over and read the credit box, and I would say, "Oh, that cinematographer, Caleb Deschanel, who shot this movie . . . didn't he also shoot *The Black Stallion*?" And then I'd go find *The Black Stallion* and read the credit box. "Oh, it was!" There wasn't Google, so you couldn't plug in his name and see what other movies he had done. That was my IMDb: physically walking around the store and matching names.

Niche genres found a comfortable home on video store shelves, such as these at Vidiots.

Joe Swanberg: I didn't know how to find other Coen brothers movies other than going into the video store and turning over every box and looking at the credits block until I found their names. So, when I turned over *The Hudsucker Proxy* and saw Joel Coen, it was this incredible moment that was the culmination of all this searching. Here was this treasure I found.

Greg Mottola: I had a class with Andrew Sarris on Hitchcock and Orson Welles at Columbia. He would show us a film, usually more obscure ones, every week, alternating between the directors. My friends and I would go to the video store and seek out the ones he wasn't showing in class.

Nicole Holofcener: Working at the store was an education. I hadn't known about Roman Polanski. We'd watch them and copy them, and you could own your own movies. The covetousness had such a strange effect on everybody. We all wanted to own them. I remember discovering Neil Simon and falling in love with Henry Jaglom's early movies, like *Can She Bake a Cherry Pie?* and that one about ducks that his brother was in. It confirmed how much I loved movies and how much I loved talking about movies. And how much I wanted to work on them.

Alex Ross Perry: A film student today doesn't have the curated collection of DVDs that I, and all of my friends, had at home. I am sure that the average film student doesn't come to his dorm with a hundred and fifty DVDs that he has to make room for.

J.C. Chandor: When I went to NYU, that was when I first dove into Kim's, during the summer of '93. I would do a whole director at a time and watch all their stuff. I would feel behind the curve of people who had seen everything. That place was the great equalizer; it had every great filmmaker. The whole place was a little bit beyond me, but in the best possible way. It forced me to dive in to find out what I didn't know.

Greg Mottola: I went into that phase of watching John Waters, Roger Corman, and early Jonathan Demme. All of that stuff, I discovered in video stores. Even the more conventional video store would have an indie section, and you could find that stuff and you could connect it to people in the underground world. It would lead tendrils back to the sixties and the seventies—to Kenneth Anger, Stan Brackhage.

Luc Besson: After I did my first film, *The Last Combat*, the first critique I got in a newspaper, the guy said that I was referring to three films. I was very flattered someone was talking about me in a newspaper. But I had never seen those three films. I read it and I didn't understand anything. I couldn't recognize my film. So I ran to the video store because I thought, maybe I'll understand something. So I went to the store to buy a VCR. The first time I went to the video club was to rent the films that had apparently inspired me. One was Tarkovsky's *Andrei Rublev*. The two others, I don't remember. I watched the Tarkovsky, and it is a great film, but I still don't understand the relationship with mine. After I discovered the video club was next to where I lived in Paris, I was there every day.

Kevin Smith: At RST Video, during the day, it was pretty mild at work. When you were working, you never stopped the movie, you could still listen to it and chances are it's *Blue Velvet* for the forty-sixth time and so you know the movie without even looking at it. But all that dialogue is seeping into your head. My feeling was that I learned to write dialogue because I listened to movies more than I looked at them. My movies didn't look very good because I didn't really look up at the TV. It wasn't until later that I improved on visuals, which I should have done, because it's a visual medium. But I think I came in so dialogue-heavy because I had spent years just listening to movies.

John Sayles: When I was in school, there wasn't a film program, but there was a professor who would show all of Ingmar Bergman's movies, and he had this special cold light prism projector so that he could stop on a still frame, so the film wouldn't melt. That was a big deal. We could work through a movie and stop. Quentin Tarantino's generation didn't go to film school either, but with video they could stop a movie or run it backwards. I say to students, "Take a film you love and run it without sound." How did this guy put that film together? That aspect is something that was not really available before video. You can watch it over and over again. You can stop frames. It has been an enormous filmmaking tool.

Kevin Smith: The video store was the beginning of everything. It was the cradle of civilization. It was like living in a film library. You could watch anything, and you could watch it over and over again. That was the beginning of repeat watching.

Joe Swanberg: For better or worse, I am from a generation that very much wants to consume and reconsume its own shit. And so the video store, for me growing up, was like access to everything and access to watch and rewatch shit. Unfortunately, what happens to my generation is, we don't just watch *Breakfast Club* two times while it's in movie theaters. We watch *Breakfast Club* sixty-nine times between the age of twelve and twenty-five, and we convince ourselves that *The Breakfast Club* is a genius movie. You have this wrapped up nostalgia and regurgitation and overconsumption of mediocre shit. It is really annoying to me. It is a bad direction that our culture is going in. And I directly tie that to the video store. We had every movie ever made available to us to freeze-frame and scroll through and totally overanalyze. Movies aren't meant to be held up to that level of scrutiny. Most aren't. The ability to know and study every shot of a movie until you know it by heart is not necessarily great. Not like being inspired by something and making your own art from it. It becomes heady and intellectual rather than emotional. You actually remember them better if you sort of misremember them.

John Sayles: Yeah, but you had the appreciation the first time. You got that thrill.

Morgan Spurlock: How many times have I seen *It's a Wonderful Life*? I know what's gonna happen every time that movie plays, and I cry at the end of that movie. So I don't know if dissecting things makes me not be affected by them emotionally.

David O. Russell: Anybody I meet, I say, "Take twenty or thirty minutes of a film and memorize it." *Chinatown;* I could tell it to you right now like you're watching the movie. It starts out before Jake Gittes goes to the orange grove. He goes to the land deed office, and he coughs to rip the page. You know what I'm talking about? I could do the whole thing if you want me. The story is hurtling forward. So I memorized that. I live it. If I did it for you right now, you would get from me the experience of almost someone acting out that section of the film. I wouldn't just be mathematically calculative. The only way I know how to feel stories and write stories is by me telling it to you, as if I was telling you a story over coffee and I had to hold your attention. With *The Fighter*, the script wasn't done, the one that I was involved in helping rewrite. All the way up to production, the studio was nervous. Same thing with *American Hustle*. And how do I keep the financers from losing it when their lawyers are saying, "This is not cool. You don't have a final script in your hand." I come into their conference rooms, I say, "OK, listen. I'm gonna recite it to you." I tell them the movie just like I would tell *Chinatown*.

Clerk Life

"The store was my Village Voice *and I was the Andrew Sarris."*

Quentin Tarantino: I found Video Archives in Manhattan Beach and I thought the place was the coolest place I had ever seen in my life. After going there for a little time, I was flat on my ass, wondering what I would do. I needed a job, and I was trying to get out of sales jobs when you just work by commission.

Kevin Smith: My mother was up my ass, "You got to get a job." That summer, 1989, I went through three. I worked at Domino's for one day and I never came back. They made me wear slacks, and I look terrible in slacks. I went to work at a cemetery. And they asked me to dig a fucking grave. Right then and there, I was like, "I am too young." And I worked at an Italian bakery, which you'd imagine I'd love, but I hate Italian pastries.

Quentin Tarantino: [In 1985,] the owner asked if I wanted to have a job there. He didn't realize how much he was saving my life. And for three years, it was really great. The case could be made that it was really too terrific. I lost all my ambition for the first three years. I stopped trying to act and trying to direct.

Kevin Smith: So I am combing the want ads. And I see the dream job. "Help wanted. Video store." And I go to RST [in New Jersey], and we sit behind the counter on these little footstools. So our chins are at counter height. That was the first thing that charmed me. I was like, "Look at this shit, we're living like children, surrounded by movies. We'll never grow old and we'll never die. This is the *Cocoon* of jobs."

Nicole Holofcener: I was going to NYU and a video store called New Video opened up in my neighborhood on University Place. I worked there on and off for a year. It was so fun. I loved talking about movies and learning about them. I got to take home stacks of movies and watch them over and over again, and to copy them, of course, to start my own collection. It was a whole movie culture.

Curation, such as clerks' picks sections, helped define video store culture.

Kevin Smith: I didn't want to be a filmmaker. I had no plans that this would be my training ground. I just wanted to work at a video store. It seemed like the best place in the world. I thought I was going to be sitting behind the counter on a little footstool for the rest of my life. And brother, that suited me just fine. My father hated his job at the post office. He worked nights as a letter carrier. He would have me call in sick for him. I saw how having a job he hated affected my old man. Here was a job I loved, and I got it.

Quentin Tarantino: I was very good at it. I could definitely push the stuff that I liked, or what I thought was interesting and challenging. I made fans of some very weird stuff. For the most part, I tried to gear it for the customer. A housewife comes and, say, she wants something. I am twenty-four and she's fifty-four, so I'm not going to try to give her *Eraserhead* or *Forbidden Zone* or some kung fu movie. If she likes Tom Hanks? I am not going to steer her toward *Bachelor Party*, but I could very well steer her toward *Nothing in Common*. "Have you seen *Nothing in Common* with Tom Hanks and Jackie Gleason?" "No, I haven't seen that one." "That's perfect for you." It's not perfect for me but perfect for her. I was pretty good that way.

Kevin Smith: I always liked being in the video store and being helpful, and I'd try to tell people what to rent even if it was the same stupid shit over and over again. I was like, "I get it, dude. Movies. Who gives a fuck what they are." I loved talking with people. There was no Internet, so you couldn't jump on a message board or Twitter. "This is what I loved about *Guardians of the Galaxy*. I am Groot! *#fuckin'thismovierocks*." You didn't get to do that. You gotta do that in person with people.

Quentin Tarantino: Me and the other guys would walk into the local movie theater and we'd be heading toward our seats and we'd hear, "There go the guys from Video Archives." We were known all over that town. In a strange way, Video Archives in Manhattan Beach was a primer to what it would be like to be famous. Everyone in Manhattan Beach knew who I was. I couldn't walk down the street without people calling, "Hey, Quentin. Hey, Quentin!"

Joe Swanberg: We were ordering fifteen films a day for the store, and the manager didn't care. She was like, "Yeah, whatever. Here's the password to order what you want." The little store in Naperville, Illinois, this corporate video store, had a massive foreign film section. It had a massive documentary section.

Quentin Tarantino: A lot of non–foreign film fans were drawn to the films of Eric Rohmer because Eric Rohmer boxes were very, very sexy, especially that *Pauline at the Beach* box from the connoisseur section. The video box is her ass in a swimsuit. People would come up with different Eric Rohmer movies, like *Chloe in the Afternoon*. Chris Rock made a remake of *Chloe in the Afternoon*, and he said the only reason he picked up the video in the first place was because the box looked so sexy. I was a fan of Eric Rohmer. And so they would come over and say, "Hey, is this any good?" And I say, "Well, it's an Eric Rohmer movie." And they say, "Who's that?" And I say, "Well, he's a French director and he makes these amusing little morality tales, little parables that usually star a bunch of young people in and around Paris." So, they ask, "They're comedies?" "No, they're not comedies. But they are slightly amusing the way everything ends up playing out. I like them. I like the way they play out. Some people might think they are boring. You have to commit to watching it, to let them get to where they get to. They're minor. But if you get a taste for it, it can become very satisfying." And that worked. Almost everybody I said that to watched those movies and watched them in the right way with the right expectations, whereas they might have turned them off after fifteen minutes if they didn't hear my little spiel. And they would come back and rent the other Eric Rohmer movies. Before long, all of our Eric Rohmer movies had rented eighty times.

Nicole Holofcener: It's very personal renting videos to people. For the porn section, it's like, "Okay, you are into taboo sex. You keep renting the taboo series." I would say, "Yeah, I heard this one is really good. You're going to like it. Tell me how it came out." Some horrible, inappropriate joke.

Kevin Smith: Of course there was porn at RST. And it was stocked, son. Blockbuster never did porn, and so the mom-and-pops stayed in business with their porn rooms. Watching people interact with the porn room was awesome. Once you get comfortable with people, they wouldn't do this dance, "Oh, what's in the kids' section? Ah, this looks good." Pick up a drama. And then saunter back to the porn room and reach for the filthiest thing on the planet and then have to bring it up to the counter with *Turner and Hooch*. It was one of the particular joys of the video store.

Nicole Holofcener: I had a really big crush on this

actor. He wasn't famous, but he was well known and he rented a lot of movies. And then one day he rented gay porn.

Kevin Smith: Now, you can pop open your computer and look at any kind of pornography. But back then, it was like, "Look at all these boxes!" People would smoke to the counter, looking out the window, making sure no one else is coming. There was one lady, a married mom. She had to be maybe forty-five. She would rent the action movie, the kids' movie, and a hardcore flick. She just got down to, "Just give me what's new." Once you're comfortable with someone renting porn, you can have conversations with him or her. Having a frank conversation with someone about his or her sex life informed my work a great deal.

Nicole Holofcener: Kent Jones, who's now the head of the New York Film Festival, was the film-buff, archivist clerk at the store. And there was another guy who was the porn expert. Of course, I ended up dating that guy, which was a big mistake.

Kevin Smith: If you had the eleven o'clock shift, nothing would be happening until three o'clock when the kids got out of school. Sometimes you'd lock the door and put up the "in the bathroom" sign and go into the porno room and just turn around and do a three-sixty and tug one out. "Look at all this free pornography! Pictures everywhere!" The hottest thing I ever did at RST Video was have sex with a girl in the porno room. Usually, when I was in the room, it was me with my dick in my hand. So the dream of being in the porno room and having sex with a real person, I was able to make come true.

Quentin Tarantino: The store was my *Village Voice* and I was the Andrew Sarris. At a certain point I got to know everyone's taste. And after three years, it got to be a real drag putting movies in people's hands. I just wanted to do my job. But people got so used to, "So, Quentin, what am I going to get today?" They wanted the whole treatment. That was fun the first three years but not so fun the last two years. The last year, I would almost roll my eyes when someone would walk through the door. "Oh, shit, I've got to talk to this guy. I'm working a minimum-wage job, I want to get out of here." You know, the McDonald's guy doesn't have to talk about every hamburger to everybody that comes in. When I started getting sick of the place, I started to reconnect with my ambition.

Kevin Smith: I was not the rude clerk. Bryan [Johnson, who also worked at RST Video] is a creature of pride. To serve anybody is not in his matrix. It makes his skin crawl. To have to serve people whom he considers of lesser intelligence—to kowtow to someone who's renting *Problem Child* instead of a good David Lynch movie—that would drive Bryan nuts.

Nicole Holofcener: A woman I worked with at New Video, Lora Hirschberg, was very mean to me. She had a really dry, sarcastic sense of humor, and I was really intimidated by her. I was the new girl. She became this brilliant sound mixer up at Skywalker. We ran into each other. And she said, "I love your movies. Do you remember me?" We have worked things out. She does an amazing job on my movies, which I would not normally be able to afford.

Morgan Spurlock: When you're in film school, you're with people who try and one-up one another with who can talk about the most obscure Buñuel film. So everybody went to Kim's. I walked in there, and it was what you would imagine. Nobody speaks to you; nobody says "Welcome," or "Hey," or "Welcome to Kim's video." You walk in and you are invisible. Not only are you invisible, but it's like you're an asshole for walking in. And so I asked a question like, "Can you tell me where the new releases are?" The person made fun of me in some way. You can't help but be intimidated. I had transferred to NYU and I probably would have been twenty years old, intimidated by somebody who's not that much older than me, probably just out of NYU. Probably an angry, frustrated filmmaker.

Alex Ross Perry: If you're anointed to be the person to guard this wonderful supply of cinema, you have to make good. If you are going to be the gatekeeper and the archivist at Kim's, this three-story place, then you also have to be able to handle whatever comes in. And a lot of times, it was a bozo who would come in off the street looking for whatever new release you had in the window. Or it could be an eccentric scholar looking for something specific.

Darren Aronofsky: I never had that thing with the clerks. They were very intense, but when you talked with them, they were very helpful.

Kevin Smith: The attitude of, "Do you really want me to get up and get that movie? I have to work?" To be fair, that was just the insouciance of lower-middle-class, still-privileged white kids working at a job.

Joe Swanberg: Most video stores, it was just a college kid collecting a minimum-wage paycheck who didn't give a shit. Only a certain number of stores had those dedicated, intelligent employees.

Quentin Tarantino: If you were rude to us, we'd be rude to you, but we couldn't quite be. Our video store wasn't in the Village. It was in a nice, white suburban community, Manhattan Beach, with parents whose kids were all surfer types. It was our job to fit in the community. We couldn't be cooler than thou. It was our job to fit into the upper-middle-class community. As it was, the store became incredibly popular. They couldn't believe they had such a cool store.

We resented all of the other cool video stores in L.A. because we thought our video store was fifteen times better, and they were all in cool locations, like Rocket Video in Hollywood. Vidiots was around. They all fucking sucked. The only store that could hold a candle to us was Mondo Video, and they went out of business. They were stuck in San Pedro forever. They were like us.

At one point, I brought all of the employees together to talk with them about an employee takeover. "Let's put all our money together and buy out Lance's side of the store, and then we'll own the store with Dennis." Now, none of us had any money, but this was a legitimate business thing. "Go to your parents and borrow the six thousand dollars, you and you and you and you. This is all legit." Nobody was interested. I loved the place. I was really, really invested in it. The truth of the matter is, if we had done that, I may not have made *Reservoir Dogs*. I would have been working at, and owning, Video Archives.

Nicole Holofcener: He was at Sundance when I had *Walking and Talking* (1996) there. I remember hearing he worked in a video store. But I felt he was so much smarter about movies than I could ever be, so he could have that legend. He could have that.

The Indie-Horror Paradigm

"It was a sneak peek at the craft."

Alex Ross Perry: I was a cliché teenage boy with very few friends. And horror spoke to me.

Tim Blake Nelson: How I started to learn film language was through two seemingly opposing but actually quite related film classes. One formal and the other completely informal. The formal one was in the semiotics department, where I took semiotics and film history courses. They were obsessed with Hitchcock. And the informal one was, every Thursday night, my buddies and I would get a horror movie, like a cheap one like *Bloodsucking Freaks*. We were learning the basics of film language; how music, composition, camera movement, color timing, use of light, and casting could conspire dramatically to scare the shit out of you. Or, in the case of Semiotics 66, to create a sense of tension through Hitchcock films. The vocabulary was very easy to get your mind around. Seeds were being planted, but I just didn't understand that.

Joe Swanberg: I watched a lot of horror in a studying kind of way. I was really into Troma [*Toxic Avenger, Class of Nuke 'Em High*] when I was a kid. Those were the most inspirational and most influential movies, because you could see how they were made. They were their own film school because they demystified the process. "Oh, I can see the tube where the blood is spurting out." There was not a lot of movie magic happening there. It was a sneak peek at the craft. It was also a lot of naked girls.

Alex Ross Perry: It just was fun. I mean, I got out of it what you're supposed to get out of it, which was fear and excitement and titillation, and also there just was a lot of it. And it was really easy for me to understand, if I saw *Halloween*, that I then had seven other movies that I would probably enjoy in some way that

I could rent next. My parents couldn't care less about what I was consuming in any way, because it obviously made me happy and I had nothing else to do.

Darren Aronofsky: In the video stores, the weird stuff would sit on the shelves and just wait there and wouldn't go anywhere. They wouldn't take them down.

Ted Hope: There wasn't classic cinema yet available in many of the video stores. It took a little while for that to happen. A lot of it was just, "Put whatever on the shelf that you can get."

Morgan Spurlock: You could actually watch something over and over and over again, and it was awesome. The amount of times I would go frame by frame through *Scanners* and watch the guy's head explode—it was spectacular. The amount of times I went frame by frame through *An American Werewolf in London* and watched his snout grow or watched his hands grow, was phenomenal. For me, as a kid who loved movies, this was a chance to really study them.

Ted Hope: I would watch Roger Corman films [*House of Usher*, *The Wild Angels*, *Piranha*] and early film noir, partly just looking for how to make movies cheaply, yet dynamic.

John Sayles: Roger took a year's vacation after selling New World, around 1984, and when he came back he realized the big studios were making his genre movies and they were spending fifty million dollars, so he couldn't compete with them. So he went to making straight-to-video movies.

Darren Aronofsky: Troma and those underground B-movies—the weird, horror, sci-fi exploitation thing—that became a big part of that whole video thing because the video stores had them all. There was a stage when we were watching those films for the scares and the nudity because we were teenagers. I am sure it influenced me.

David O. Russell: The films I rented a lot were *Night of the Living Dead* and *Re-Animator*. The first screenplay I wrote was a horror film. But to be honest with you, it's not in my blood. It's in Quentin's blood. It was a path to getting out of my day job. I just wanted to try something, so I wrote a horror film.

Ted Hope: Of the films I cut my teeth on, I would have to say most of the films of my PA days and slightly beyond were driven by video deals more than anything else. A film that was very influential to me in my producing was called *Doom Asylum* (1987).

Alex Ross Perry: *Halloween*'s an independent, low-budget movie. You're looking at movies that are made with incredibly limited resources, which is really important when you're fourteen and you're working in a TV studio in high school. No one talks about horror movies as being independent movies. I mean, they do, but not a hundred percent of the time. But—look at almost all American horror from the sixties and seventies. It's low-budget, grindhouse filmmaking. That's independent filmmaking.

John Sayles: You can always find some crummy old house and kill people in it. There is a real use of camera and attention to cutting and mood and suggestion, especially when you don't have much money. You have to manufacture it in the filmmaking. For *Piranha*, I wrote the angles in the shooting scripts, "blood churning in the water, cut to piranhas," specifically and rhythmically. You have to think about it a lot. You can see it in *Brother from Another Planet*. It's not a scary movie, but in the first ten minutes, there is almost no dialogue. You're building the storytelling the same way you might with creepy music.

Ted Hope: Steve Menkin, a friend, called me because they had put together a hundred thousand dollars to make *Doom Asylum*, but they didn't have a script or a cast. They had to shoot in four weeks because of the delivery date. We basically ran actor friends of ours up and down an abandoned insane asylum's hallways. We used techniques like shooting in a location you can control; use natural lighting wherever possible; trying to use youthful characters because they're non-SAG and you could afford them; cover things in as few shots as possible, so you're not doing dolly moves; doing walk-and-talks to the camera, or away from the camera, that sort of stuff. These became the Good Machine No-Budget Commandments. [Good Machine was the production company behind *The Brothers McMullen*, *The Ice Storm*, *In the Bedroom* and other breakout independents.] It's not how people dreamed of making movies: It was filmmaking by necessity. We would sit around and talk about this. And [friend and aspiring director] Hal Hartley listened carefully and took all of that to design *The Unbelievable Truth*.

Stocking the Shelves

"They were getting acquired, essentially, with home video money."

Ted Hope: There wouldn't be an American independent film business unless there had been a scarcity of content available for the American video shelf. Period.

Kevin Smith: There was a voracious marketplace of people getting off their nine-to-five jobs, grabbing the kids from school and going to the video store, and then going home. This was the daily ritual. I saw some cats three times a day. Somebody asking,

"Did *Young Guns* get returned yet?" I was like, "Dude, as soon as it's in, I'm calling you."

Ted Hope: They had pretty predictive formulas on how films would succeed. They couldn't predict the hits, but they could predict the base, which, to have predictive revenues, allowed everything.

Ira Deutchman: Even if the film was bad, they knew they could do a certain number of units on video. That had to do with cast. It also had to do with horror films and certain genres, like thrillers.

Darren Aronofsky: That was the amazing thing about those video stores; they pretty much bought everything. They filled those shelves, and they brought in more and more videotapes.

Richard Gladstein: The horror genre didn't rely on name actors, per se. And these movies often didn't require a theatrical release in order to achieve video revenues, whereas most films did. For most films, there was a direct correlation between what it did in the theater to what it did on video. But certain genres, because the video market was flourishing, so many people were going to video stores, video companies like LIVE began to make horror films that would just go direct to video.

Ted Hope: For the longest period, there were just tons and tons of crap video stores. My memory is seeing Roy Scheider's *52 Pick-Up* everywhere; every time going to the store and saying, "Well, I guess we could watch this again. At least it's done well."

Richard Gladstein: We did the sequels for *Howling*, *Children of the Corn*, *Silent Night, Deadly Night*; these kind of movies that were not intended to be released theatrically. We would always figure forty bucks a tape was our profit and we would sell them for $56 a store. So you take off the duplication and marketing costs, etc.. When I was running my numbers, if forty bucks a tape was my profit, if you could sell 40,000 units, that's 1.6 million, and so I'll spend 1.2 million on the movie. Roughly, those were the numbers. *Silent Night, Deadly Night*—if I sell 30,000 units, that's a 1.2 in profit. And I'll spend $900,000.

Ira Deutchman: There was a period of time that lasted perhaps ten years when I used to joke that anything with the sprocket holes that was in English could sell to home video. That was what financed our entire operation. There was this enormous boom of money that was available, strictly driven by the home video businesses' appetite to fill up all of those shelves in the mom–and–pop stores, in order to be able to justify memberships. They needed to stock their shelves up. They needed to look like they had a lot of different titles. Somebody had to do that, and the studios were not supplying enough product.

Richard Gladstein: There was the old saying, "I made a poster, then I made a movie." What you really did was you made the video box and then you filled it. I made whatever I wanted. I had greater ambitions, but we knew how to fill the box. Because that distribution medium was earning so much money, there were some home video companies that stepped into the void of financing. It became not just a market for releasing. Essentially, there were some home video companies like RCA and LIVE Entertainment that arose because video rights were so extraordinarily valuable. We often partnered or financed a large portion of films in exchange for the distribution rights.

Ira Deutchman: I refer to it as, "The independent bubble." I don't think it was ever a real marketplace. I think it was something that was built on a lot of smoke and mirrors. And somehow justified itself on an ongoing basis. In the same way that there was a real estate bubble, and there was an Internet bubble. This independent bubble happened as a result of there being so much money in the marketplace from home video.

John Pierson: The companies that were buying the available titles from the independent companies were just competing to piss their money away.

Ira Deutchman: We became founders of a brand-new independent company, called Cinecom. The idea behind Cinecom was that we were going to take the smaller marketing techniques that had been used mainly for foreign-language films in the United States. Every single studio had a classics division at that time. We couldn't compete for the foreign-language films. Ironically, those were the films that were being bid up to ridiculous proportions. As a new startup without a whole lot of money, we really couldn't compete in that realm.

John Pierson: There was a changeover from subtitled world cinema being the artsy, non-studio thing that people might go to see to American independent films. That was very much, if not entirely, fueled by the then-burgeoning home video industry, which was extremely biased against foreign-language films. Even to this day, people don't really like watching subtitles on their big TVs. On *Slacker*, we were disappointed when our first run was seven thousand video-cassettes. As an illustration of what foreign could do, we were told at the time that that's how the most successful Almodóvar movie sold on video. It was bleak.

Ira Deutchman: There was this burgeoning, independent movement that we were hearing about. There had just been the first IFP (Independent Film Project) market [in 1979]. The term "independent" was being used around John Sayles's *Secaucus* 7, and a couple of other films that were out. We thought, "Maybe we can use the same marketing methods that had been used for foreign-language films and point audiences towards these American independent films, and see if we can make something out of that."

John Sayles: When it was happening, we caught the wave. We got money for films. It was clear we were not going to go with the studios, because they were not interested in the movies we were making. And these could be independent movies made like independent movies, where there weren't a million story conferences and compromises. And we were not spending that much. It was a great second wind. We had been out there raising money in limited partnerships from friends and family and independents, but it never got more than three- or four hundred thousand dollars. Suddenly, we could make a movie for three million dollars rather than three hundred thousand.

Ira Deutchman: We started acquiring some movies. The first of which was *Come Back to the Five and Dime, Jimmy Dean, Jimmy Dean* (1982). Then it was Gillian Armstrong's *Starstruck* (1982). The studios were not really supplying a lot of product to the home video market, so we became incredibly valuable. We bought *El Norte* (1983), *The Brother from Another Planet* (1984), *Stop Making Sense* (1984). Our biggest hit was *A Room With a View* (1985). Which ended up doing something like twenty-three million dollars box office.

John Pierson: '85 to '95 is the decade when there was the funny money.

Ira Deutchman: Because there was so much money flooding the marketplace from the home video business, it meant that a lot of independent films got made that would not have gotten made otherwise. That's when independent film got its name. Because, suddenly, there seemed like there was a business. There was financing available. It was not just home video, but home video was definitely central to it. We would know that as long as we spent a certain amount of money to market films, that it would trigger an automatic deal with the home video company that would net us more than we spent. What it did was it emboldened us to go out and spend more money, both to acquire movies as well as to market movies. It also incentivized us, by the way, to overspend on the marketing. That overspending, even for a film that we knew wasn't going to work theatrically, would trigger a home video sale that would end up bailing us out, essentially.

Richard Gladstein: We did really, really well. *Drug Store Cowboy* (1989), we'd put up forty percent of the budget, two million dollars, for the video rights—but you, Avenue Pictures, you have to warrant to us that you will release it in *x* amount of markets. And we knew that if they would release it in that way, with advertising and promotion, it would be advertising for our six-months-later video window.

Ira Deutchman: As a result of home video, theatrical became a loss leader. During my Fine Line years [*My Own Private Idaho*, *Naked*, *Short Cuts*, etc.], which would have been in the nineties, the idea was that the more profile that you created theatrically, it would create value that would eventually accrue to the benefit of the film, but mostly on home video. It was the tail wagging the dog. Home video was the deciding factor in an enormous number of decisions that were being made both creatively and otherwise. And it was just about everything that we released.

Richard Gladstein: As a video company, we had to release thirty-six films a year, three films a month. We would get a couple of films from Carolco, our parent company. We would get a few from output deals. We'd get a bunch from Miramax. That would leave us with fifteen to eighteen a year that we had to in some way acquire. Most of those were one-offs from film festivals or from producers, or we would make the sequels to horror films. As we were doing that, because my interest was in other genres, we began to provide financing to what became independent art films. We provided money to *King of New York* (1990), *Bob Roberts* (1992), and *Bad Lieutenant* (1992). Personally, those were movies that I had a greater interest in. Avenue Pictures, Cary Brokaw's company, was making movies like *Drugstore Cowboy* and *After Dark, My Sweet* (1990), and our company provided the lion's share of the budgets in exchange for the video rights. Movies got financed because the revenue stream became so valuable.

Ira Deutchman: We would sit in meetings at New Line when we were deciding whether to green-light a movie or not. The key piece of information that would indicate whether the film was going to get made or not, had to do with the number of home video units that the stars of the contemplated film had done on prior films. Whether it was a self-fulfilling prophecy or not is a good question.

Richard Gladstein: I should say that there was a company called RCA/Columbia, which was run by Larry Estes. I was in some ways mimicking what he was doing.

Doug Liman: There was a market at the time—you could make smaller movies that wouldn't go theatrical. That was my first opportunity to make a movie. [1994's *Getting In*, a straight-to-video movie, was Liman's directorial debut.] There were opportunities for filmmakers starting out to actually have a job making a movie financed through home video sales. My particular career trajectory depended on home video entertainment.

Greg Mottola: Money could be made there. Pre-sales could happen. Financially, it was one of the ways that was allowing indie films to flourish in its particular way in the nineties.

Doug Liman: I raised the money for *Swingers* (1996) from a friend of my father's, so I felt the moral obligation that what I was doing made business sense but [was] also a familial obligation. It made a big difference that, as a fallback, there was a chance to sell the movie to home video. You could look an investor straight in the eyes and say, "This is a pretty safe investment." I knew if I finished, that a film shot on 35 mm, in color, and with sync sound—that it had a certain value on home video regardless of its quality, and that that value exceeded the amount of money I'd raised to make it.

Ted Hope: I think *Trust* (1990) is one of the stronger under $1 million dollar movies. Every frame in it is dynamic, so it translates very well to a television screen. You're not found wanting a bigger frame. I don't think it was so much conscious, but really the aesthetics of necessity. It's just this happy accident, because when you shoot per a low budget, you're not really making a detailed frame. You're making a frame that you're still really trying to make dynamic, but you're really populating it with faces and a decent angle.

Doug Liman: A film like *Swingers*, which was made for a small amount of money with a camera that was on my shoulder, probably plays better on home video than it does in a theater. The theatrical experience is more about visual spectacle.

David O. Russell: That was the bubble. We were in the middle of this massive safety net where you could finance a movie out of video sales. There was so much money in them. It was like the Clinton expansion. That's how I got to do everything. There was a great feeling of, "I could take a risk on this, because we have a video net."

David O. Russell on set. *Joy* ©2015. Twentieth Century Fox. All rights reserved.

Quentin Tarantino: From 1988 to 1992, people were all of a sudden getting $800,000—or a million, or a million point two—to make their little genre movie.

Ira Deutchman: Every single thing we did went through that analysis, in terms of whether their films would have gotten made or distributed. It would have been everybody from Spike Lee to John Sayles, who was definitely a creature of home video during those early years, to Jim Jarmusch, Hal Hartley, Whit Stillman, you name it. Because if those films were getting acquired, they were getting acquired, essentially, with home video money. I would say just about every young director who came of age as an independent during the eighties would probably be in that category.

The Man with the Keys

"Big, big, big, big impact . . ."

Quentin Tarantino: Everyone was trying to get to Larry Estes. He was the one with the keys. He was the cool guy.

Ira Deutchman: RCA/Columbia handled all of the home video for the Columbia labels. It's an indication of how, in the early days, nobody understood that home video would become such a big business, so there were all sorts of strange partnerships that cropped up. They were a very important transitional company because they were essentially admitting to themselves that there was no way that the studios could supply the product that they needed. They needed stuff that they could feed into their system. RCA/Columbia was leading the charge on the independent side of the spectrum. When I first met Larry, he was working in non-theatrical sales for Films Incorporated, out of their Atlanta office. Then he moved into home video. He moved to L.A. and became the independent guy at RCA/Columbia home video. He was responsible for a lot of the deals.

Quentin Tarantino: We had met with a bunch of people, but never as big as Larry Estes and RCA/Columbia. We never met with anyone like *that*.

Larry Estes: I was functioning at the time like someone who was the miniature studio in the back of the big studio approving casts and directors and looking at budgets and certainly the script. I started with three movies that were not just, "Let's buy the video rights." I figured, "Why don't I just own it and I'll pay the producer a million dollars and I'll figure out how much to spend on it." It was a negative pickup arrangement. You were making an arrangement where the producer would make the movie and take all the risks of getting it made on time for the money that was available. It was like saying, "I'll cosign your loan, and when it's completed, I am the only person to whom you would sell it." It was basically acquiring the entire movie, and the producer was the partner. The first was *Deadly Illusion* (1987), a detective movie, with Billy Dee Williams. It cost $3.5 million. I learned you don't have to spend $3.5 million. The second was directed by Bill Lustig, called *Hit List* (1989), with Rip Torn. It cost $1.5 million, and it tripled its money in the video market. *Sex, Lies, and Videotape* (1989) was the third. No one thought it was going to make a lot of money.

Ira Deutchman: I don't think that it was on anybody's radar screen that this kind of stuff was going on, other than independent producers who were looking for every source of financing that they could find.

Larry Estes: The script that we approved was even more downbeat at the end. Steven Soderbergh came to me from Outlaw Productions with a visionary guy, Bobby Newmyer. Bobby found out I liked this film *Patti Rocks* (1988). His pitch was, "How would you like to make *Patti Rocks* for less than five hundred thousand dollars? I have the script for it." That's how he got me interested. It turned out we couldn't make it for that. But when I read it, I said, "I am dying to see this movie tomorrow, so let's do this. It is unusual and out there. And we have the money." It turned out to be more of an art film than even I thought.

Richard Gladstein: They were making *Sex, Lies, and Videotape*, but I couldn't do a straight drama, an obvious art film. The drama genre does not sell well at the video store.

Larry Estes: Unusual is okay if it's sexy. We all felt like it was unlike anything we had read. We hoped *Sex, Lies* would make us twenty or thirty percent on our money. We hoped to make a million back, and then another two or three hundred thousand, and we would have been happy. In the late eighties, if something had sexual content, you were almost guaranteed to make a certain amount of money. It wasn't as risky as two guys going off to have a dinner conversation. That was a movie at the time.

Ira Deutchman: They got the money they needed to make the movie. When the film went to Sundance, they hired me to rep the film and to find them distribution. But RCA/Columbia owned it. We made the deal with Miramax. What really shocked people was that Miramax would buy a movie without home video rights. It was already pretty clear that home video, for independent films especially, was an enormous chunk of the value of the movie. Harvey [Weinstein] took that risk, and it paid off for him.

Larry Estes: It became more viewer-friendly, but until Sundance, we didn't think it would be anything more than another video movie that we put out for a million bucks. But after that, producers started to feel, "Now I don't have to just make movies with a bloody knife and a partially clad woman on the video box to get a deal. I can start doing riskier and edgier stuff. This is where I can go to get money. In the past, I had to go to a bunch of dentists and convince them they'd make money on my independent film." I was being offered things in the *Sex, Lies* area before, but I hadn't felt like I could justify it. I would have to pitch the films to the boss, and the sales people who would look for a reason to say no.

John Pierson: Big, big, big, big impact for those years.

Larry Estes: After *Sex, Lies* happened, everybody that made independent films came to me. The first ones I wanted to make were John Sayles's *City of Hope* (1991) and *Passion Fish* (1992), and Allison Anders's film, *Gas, Food, Lodging* (1992). I made sixty of these movies in four years. That included *One False Move* (1992), with director Carl Franklin and Billy Bob Thornton, and *Zebra Head* (1992) with Michael Rappaport and executive-produced by Oliver Stone.

John Sayles: Larry had a nice mandate. And he wanted to like the movies he was making. It wasn't just about making the top dollar but also, "Who is going to do the best job for this movie?" The bigger thing was a successful title.

Allison Anders on the set of 1992's *Gas, Food, Lodging*.

Allison Anders: We went to Larry with the pitch trying to sell him on it. I was in there with all of my male producers. And Larry had one female assistant. I had never done this before. His coverage was half-

and-half on the script. It was an unusual script at the time. He says, "Well, I have to tell you, Allison, you set us up for one thing and that doesn't happen."

Larry Estes: The script didn't have the elements that most people were looking for, so it was more like, "Please help me understand why this story is interesting to my home video audience."

Allison Anders: I didn't know what to say. I said, "I know, but that's because women's lives work like that. The male narrative is to set you up for something and you reach that goal and whatever happens, whether you win or lose, it determines what happens to him later. But with women, we set goals, but we have collected so much stuff along the way, and so much experience, that the outcome doesn't really matter." I'm talking out of my ass, by the way. And this girl is nodding her head and I'm like, "Stay with me, sister. I don't know what I'm talking about." That girl was my salvation. And Larry is just staring at me. I'm like, "I'm sorry, I've gone on a tangent." And Larry says, "No, no. That's fine. I don't know anything about women." So he says, "You go get me a budget." He was like, "Yeah." He did say, "Let me ask you about sex." I said, "Uh-oh, okay." He said, "I get these scripts with these sex scenes in them and there's all this male bravado. And then they chicken out when the time comes and they don't give me what I want."

Larry Estes: I was referring to one movie. That was *Sex, Lies, and Videotape*. In the script, it was pretty clear. I even asked Soderbergh to make sure I was reading the same script, and they were like, "Oh, yeah." When I got the last of the dailies, I thought, "Uhhh, I am in deep shit, here." It's all very carefully shot where you don't see any naughty bits. Steve's explanation was that it wasn't necessary after all. My reaction was, "How nice for you." I had some scary days going to the sales people. I was lucky it turned out to be a great movie. It became irrelevant. But going forward, I wanted to be more clear.

Allison Anders: I said, "Oh, I'll give it to you." He wanted to make sure there was some sexiness in there, especially for Ione Skye's character. It was important for me to see that as well, because of where her character had gone. It was a healing sort of thing. So while it satisfied what Larry needed for the film, it also satisfied what I needed for the character.

Quentin Tarantino: I actually wrote a movie that Larry Estes financed. It's called *Past Midnight* (1991), a *Jagged Edge* wannabe with Natasha Richardson and Rutger Hauer. I am not credited as a screenwriter, but I did a big rewrite on it.

Larry Estes: I know that Quentin was talking to a lot of other people when he was helping out on *Past Midnight*. I wasn't really offered *Reservoir Dogs* (1992). LIVE Entertainment was my competition. They made *Reservoir Dogs*.

Quentin Tarantino: RCA/Columbia never showed any interest in us. They never got in touch with us.

Larry Estes: It's embarrassing. I didn't get offered everything. For whatever reason, he got in with Richard Gladstein at LIVE. If you got in with a person whom you respected at lunch who says, "I can get this done for you," you don't necessarily go to other places. We were competitors. But we were friendly. Richard made some terrific films.

Reservoir Dogs

"Harvey Keitel with a gun."

Richard Gladstein: We hired Monte Hellman, who had directed early Roger Corman movies like *Two Lane Blacktop*, to direct a sequel to *Silent Night, Deadly Night*. And while we were doing that, Monte sent me the script for *Reservoir Dogs*.

Quentin Tarantino: What happened was that, through some mutual acquaintances, we had gotten the script to Monte Hellman. We met at C.C. Brown's. It's an ice cream parlor on Hollywood Boulevard that's not there anymore. We got together and talked. He said he really wanted to do it. I said,

"I really appreciate that. I'm a really big fan of your work. But, this one, I want to do. I wrote this for me." Monte was disappointed, but he understood and he said, "Okay, why don't you tell me how you are going to do it?" I talked about how I was going to make the movie. And he said, "Hm. I think this kid will make a really good movie. I'll tell you what, then. How about I come aboard as a producer and help you get it made?" I was like, "That is surprising. Okay, cool." He had a few avenues, but his biggest avenue was his situation with Richard at LIVE Entertainment.

Richard Gladstein: I was so taken with the script. It was bold and fresh. To me, it was my *Mean Streets*. A gritty, urban, new voice. I hoped we'd be going to Sundance. On the script, it said, "Written and directed by" on the cover. He was like, "Oh, *I'm* making the movie."

Quentin Tarantino: We only had two things, but they were legitimate. We had a good, solid script and we had a commitment from Harvey Keitel. I don't think Richard would have even read the script without Harvey Keitel attached.

Richard Gladstein: Because there was the crime element to it, I could sell it internally as a crime movie. A crime movie with Harvey Keitel.

Quentin Tarantino: Did I know about LIVE Entertainment? Of course, I did. I knew about every video company that was in America. It was all the Carolco movies, like *Rambo*, *Total Recall*. They were big. Even before he met me, he was saying, "I want to do this. I hope you choose me." We weren't used to anyone talking like that.

Richard Gladstein: The first meeting I had was with Quentin and Monte. I was like, "We are going to make this movie." They had been looking for money for a while. They jumped at the opportunity. LIVE Entertainment wasn't their first stop on the block.

Quentin Tarantino: We had some situation where we could have done it for half a million dollars. We had to pay those people off when we went with LIVE. It was a company, I think, that had a deal with a home video company.

Richard Gladstein: There was no, "Gee, I don't know, I'm going to shop around."

Quentin Tarantino: I had been a video store clerk. I knew very well that most of these movies just went straight to video. I was a bit nervous about making it with a home video company. To me, it wouldn't count if it just came out on video. It would need to get theatrical play. I wouldn't have been so into it if it were Academy Home Entertainment or Imperial Entertainment or any of these straight-to-video companies. But the fact that they were the video arm of Carolco—it was a different ball of wax. And they had their own theatrical distributor in their back pocket. They released *King of New York*; I believe it was through Seven Arts. Still, it wasn't Carolco. It didn't start with a Carolco, "C." It started with a LIVE, "L." And that was different.

Richard Gladstein: I figured, I'll couch it as, "Harvey Keitel with a gun." No one else there would read the script.

Quentin Tarantino: They were going to give us 1.3 million and it sounded pretty good. So, I ask, "What are the chances we are going to get a theatrical release with the film?" And they said, "Well, here's our situation. We can always sell it. But we have in our back pocket a distribution company that we can release our LIVE movies from. The idea is that we are making these for LIVE Video but if one is really, really good, we can go out on theatrical and we could go on the film festival circuit, and we can sell it off if we want. If we create a nice situation."

Richard Gladstein: We didn't promise. We said, "We are not saying that it will get a theatrical release. We are not a theatrical distributor ourselves, but we'll see what theatrical distributors think of the movie and we'll try to make a deal if it's in the best interest of the movie."

Quentin Tarantino: Richard was saying, "We want this to go theatrical, but if you don't pull it off, we won't."

Richard Gladstein: I basically implored my bosses at LIVE to let me finance the whole thing. I said, "I'll keep the budget really low. It won't be much more than the *Silent Night, Deadly Night* movies, and we'll own the world." I was making a lot of money for them with these horror movies. So they took a flyer on it. Instead of doing a horror movie for a million bucks, we did that for a million five and we owned the whole thing. I was able to get the financing based on that even though its aspirations were higher and the script was more unique than your usual B thriller.

And we were shooting like four months later. There were no battles. We made the movie together. We didn't give him any notes on the script. We talked about the cast. We ended up adding a little bit more money to get the actors we got. We ended up adding a little more money to extend the shooting schedule, because it looked like it was going to be something special. He was smart. He wrote for daytime, one location. He knew he wouldn't have any money. We were all a bit new at this. Quentin hadn't made a movie. But you could see that within the first days of shooting that it had the vast potential to realize something extraordinary. You could feel that in the performances of the actors.

Quentin Tarantino (left) directing Harvey Keitel in *Reservoir Dogs*. Still provided through the courtesy of Lionsgate.

Quentin Tarantino: I was shooting a lot of

film—more than what we had in the budget. I was getting good stuff. As we go into the last week, [producer] Lawrence Bender and the production manager and Richard pulled me aside and tell me, "Look, you cannot keep shooting the way you are shooting. We are going to run out of film in this last week. We have to start taking it out of the editing budget and the sound mixing budget and you're going to resent that." I said, "Well, I'm not changing the way I'm shooting. This is how I'm doing it." And Richard jumped in and said, "We like what Quentin is doing, and we are going to tell him in the last week that he has to do it different even though we love the footage and everything is going fine? No. If you need a couple of hundred thousand more, then we'll give it to you. That doesn't mean go crazy, but I am not going to make Quentin change his methodology when we like it so much." We went from 1.3, which we'd been the whole time, to 1.5.

Richard Gladstein: I am sure he would have preferred to make it for a studio. But, creatively, they may have been all over him. We had final cut but we never disagreed on anything. We could have recut it, but you look at that movie and who wants to recut it? It was looking really good.

We got into Sundance. Just getting in was a great

thrill. But being able to have five hundred people watching a movie they hadn't seen an ad or even a poster for . . . I remember putting my arm around Quentin and saying, "We'll see if someone buys the movie and if it will go to theaters, but we made a movie that we are so proud of so if nothing happens, let's not diminish what it was." For months after Sundance, straight-to-video was a distinct possibility. It took months for Miramax to buy the movie. And then we sold it.

Quentin Tarantino: I think of it as having escaped the video trap. That's how I look at it. I put my foot in the bear trap and managed to get out. The bear trap being the straight-to-video movie. Everything changed in that year, when we came out in 1992, partly because of *Reservoir Dogs*, and these other independent films that actually did find homes in theaters. They weren't sloughed off to video. A vibrant independent film movement in theaters happened.

Greg Mottola: After the blockbusters wiped out the renegade seventies generation, it seemed like there was a new way to do an end run around the mainstream. I'd lump video stores into that experience. It really felt like there was something changing in American filmmaking.

Quentin Tarantino: I didn't know any other independent filmmakers. It wasn't until I went on the film festival circuit that I started meeting all the other people who had films that year. Then, we totally felt like we were part of a movement.

Richard Gladstein: *Reservoir Dogs* grossed more in London than it did in the entire U.S. It only grossed three million dollars in the U.S. But its performance on home video was as if it had grossed twenty million. The revenue achieved on video was so incredibly vast, and continues to this day.

Quentin Tarantino: I didn't need the video store for the success of my movies. Having said that, they were crazy lucrative, magnificent, ancillary markets. *Reservoir Dogs* got a lot of attention and it did pretty good for an art film, but it didn't do as good as all the attention it got.

Follow the Money

"From came-and-went to a hit movie."

John Pierson: *Reservoir Dogs* was a case where its ongoing availability for people to watch at home was really what got it so many eyeballs.

Quentin Tarantino: We sold one hundred and fifty thousand units, which was unheard of for that small of a movie.

Larry Estes: Every twenty-five thousand units were about a million dollars. We'd bring in twenty-five thousand units, at roughly fifty-five dollars wholesale, came back about a million bucks. And that didn't count the foreign sales. *Sex, Lies* did one hundred and seventy-five thousand units the first day it sold. So we brought in seven million dollars, just on video. And that was after getting a million dollars from Miramax for theatrical and TV rights in the U.S. That was a sweet, sweet deal.

Greg Mottola: On *Daytrippers* (1996), our home video deal with Columbia Tristar was more high-end than our theatrical, which was with a preincaration of Lions Gate, called CFP. Home video money was a big chunk. We were able to pay everyone who worked on the movie back.

Tom DiCillo: I have never seen a dime from any of the DVD or VHS sales from *Johnny Suede* (1991). I don't think that this is unusual. If you talk to a lot of independent directors, the idea of ever seeing … I never saw a dime from *Living in Oblivion* (1995) from VHS.

Kevin Smith: I find it hard to believe that that didn't go into profit.

Tom DiCillo: Miramax bought the film in 1991, and they made a sale to a VHS company. And the VHS company buys it for an advance, so they may pay five hundred thousand dollars for it. They need to make that back before I see any money. And it's very easy for them to keep their books in such a way that I never see a dime. It's a black hole.

Greg Mottola: I can believe that. Once we made our deal, we never saw any money again. There were never any profits—just the initial deal.

Kevin Smith: Seven years after *Clerks* came out on video, we got a check for it. They were like, "We're in the black!" That movie cost $227,000 to pick up. I think we were in the black ten minutes after it opened. But thanks to very creative paperwork, it took seven years later before we started seeing back-end checks for *Clerks*.

Greg Mottola: I remember getting a very nice letter from Columbia Pictures explaining to me why the movie *Superbad* (2007) will never go into profit, which I find fairly funny because it was made for twenty million dollars, and between DVD and worldwide theatrical it made hundreds of millions of dollars. They have all of these creative ways to claim that the money needs to be split up on all the things that lose money and the operation of the studio.

Quentin Tarantino: In the case of *Pulp Fiction* (1994), it was doing really well and it was coming out sooner than later on video. And I wouldn't let them. I said, "No. We're not going to come out on video for an entire year." The point being that everyone was talking about the movie. And I knew how video stores worked. Yes, the cool video stores knew about the movie. But the moms-and-pops, they didn't know shit. We needed six months of customers walking in asking about *Pulp Fiction*. And then we'd announce it. And then everyone would know about *Pulp Fiction*. It was one of the biggest video releases of the year. The pre-orders broke records. The entire time, Disney was saying, "Quentin is fucking us up." I was like, "Guys, I'm using the Walt Disney model: Keep it away, keep it away." They had no choice. Harvey [Weinstein] was saying, "Whatever Quentin wants." And it worked like a dream.

Darren Aronofsky: *Requiem for a Dream* (2000) did maybe ten million worldwide, but that DVD went everywhere. A lot more people than a ten-million-dollar audience have seen that film. That was a big part of its life.

Nicole Holofcener: I was thrilled that my film could have a life after theatrical distribution. That was completely new. A whole new way to have your movie seen was opening up. I still get checks from *Walking and Talking*.

Allison Anders: To me, it felt like the theatrical was like someone is coming to my concert and the video is like they bought the record, so that they can listen to it whenever they want. I thought, "This is great. People can actually see it if they missed it in the theater."

John Sayles: We were getting paid not by how many people rented it but by how many units. Blockbuster had a formula, based on how much it grossed theatrically, and they would look at the first three or four weeks and they would determine how many units they would order. So they would order just a few of our movies. And you get to the store and they're all out, but there's a whole wall of Schwarzenegger movies.

Doug Liman: When *Swingers* came out theatrically, I went out to the 8 p.m. show on Friday night to the theater on 84th and Broadway. It was the first time I saw something that I had made with a paying audience. Halfway through the movie, the film broke. They had to refund everyone their money. And they left. The theater wasn't packed in the first place. Two weeks later, the movie was out of theaters. It was gone. Dead. That was it. The film didn't catch on theatrically outside of a small group of people in New York and L.A. All that work, and it was over.

Kevin Smith: Are you kidding me? That movie made five million dollars. What else did he think that movie was ever going to be?

Doug Liman: And then the head of Buena Vista Home Video approached me and said, "We think Miramax dropped the ball, and we think there's a big audience for this movie. We are going to promote it on home video and we're going to get that audience." That's one of the top three phone calls I've ever gotten in my life. Back then, the studios would hold these two- and three-day events in Hollywood, and they would invite the owners of video stores and wine and dine them with the glitz of Hollywood. Buena Vista had a big weekend coming up in which they were bringing hundreds of video store owners to the Disney lot. And Mel Gibson, who was promoting a big movie [*Ransom*], was giving the keynote. That year, the party was at The Derby [where *Swingers* was shot] and they made the whole weekend *Swingers*-themed. As a result, they got video stores across the country to buy dozens of copies of this teeny movie.

Months later, when you went into a video store, instead of there being one or two copies of *Swingers*, which you would normally expect from a movie that made four and a half million at the box office, there were twenty copies. The impact was life-changing. It went from "came-and-went" to a hit movie. At that particular point in our history, somebody at Buena Vista Home Video could change our lives.

Kevin Smith: From an outsider's perspective, it was always an independent film that Miramax was putting out. It was a low-budget pickup. I am not making this comparison based on quality or content, but it was a west-coast version of *Clerks*. Not the story, but it was a low-budget film that Miramax picked up and turned into a fucking sensation. I always viewed that movie as successful at the multiplex. They never went huge on it. They didn't open on a thousand screens. It was still an indie release. Still, I'd definitely agree home video is where a majority of people found *Swingers*.

Kevin Smith Grabs the Mic

"These cats just know four chords. But look at what they did!"

Kevin Smith: It wasn't like we were all the same and we were all in this together. There was a multi-tiered indie world. We were on our own in New Jersey. No one was in a yoga class with Harvey Keitel's agent. I had no Lawrence Bender go-between. I had met Vincent Pereira at RST Video, and he was like, "Let me tell you about film." Vinnie was my first film school. He was the guy who explained aspect ratios to me. We started conversing. Vinnie was not just a film buff; he was the first person I met who wanted to be a filmmaker. He said, "I want to be a director." I said, "You have to be in Hollywood to do that." He's like, "What are you talking about?" I was like, "Isn't that how it works? Don't you have to be born into that business?"

I remember reading an article where Quentin was profiled for *Reservoir Dogs*. At one point he's talking about his theory of making film, and he goes, "Why would you make a movie about being a minimum-wage slave?" He was talking about how he was once going to make a movie set at a video store. This is one or two years before I made *Clerks*. I was reading it while harboring these dreams, and here's the dude who I worship, literally saying: "Who would make that movie?" I wrote about it in this pre-*Clerks* journal. I wrote that I was going to keep at it, and when *Clerks* finally played at the Angelika, I'd find Quentin and go, "You were wrong," in a weird, the-dude-wasn't-even-talking-to-you-chip-on-my-shoulder, New Jersey kind of way.

Quentin made a movie with a million bucks and movie stars. The same with *Sex, Lies*. Hal Hartley was a big hero of mine back then, but he was getting money from a few sources. I didn't believe in our stuff like that. The people I was looking up to, they were doing it solo. Sam Raimi was out there trying to put together financing for *Evil Dead* (1981) from local dentists. That captured my imagination. *Evil Dead* was pretty much financed by local dentists. Raimi was like, "Here's my script. It's the horror genre. It's proven—you can invest this much." I could never imagine walking into my dentist's office and saying, "Look at my script, it's 164 pages full of dick jokes set in a convenience store. Do you want to invest in this?" *Clerks* had to be what it was, this little punk rock movie. And people would go, "Holy shit! These cats just know four chords. But look at what they did! It's grungy, but shit, it kind of counts as a song."

All of the stories I was reading at that time were about *Together Alone* (1991), Nick Gomez's *Laws of Gravity* (1992). Greg Araki's *The Living End* (1992). For *Slacker* (1991), Richard Linklater had done it by himself with a little help from the Austin Film Society. Cats were pulling it together and shooting. I was like, "Let me do what these cats did." Robert Rodriguez, *El Mariachi* (1992), he kept it at seven thousand dollars because he never made a print.

Years before I got into film, I read about Robert Townsend making *Hollywood Shuffle* (1987). I think he was on Howard Stern, and he was talking about how he financed his movie with credit cards. That blew my hair back. I was like, "That's fucking *pos-*

sible?" I had a bunch of credit cards that I had collected. I would just apply everywhere. I was working at the video store at the time, and I was the only one who ever answered the phone. So I would write that I was making fifty thousand dollars a year at RST as a manager in 1991, 1992. And they would call to verify information: "Is this RST Video?" "Yes." "We're calling to verify financial information for a manager, Kevin Smith." I was like, "Yeah. He makes fifty grand a year." And they were like, "Thank you." I was making four bucks an hour and the store was never open for more than eight hours in the day. So do the math. I had a thirty-thousand-dollar limit with all of my credit cards. After twenty thousand, I'd be concerned, but it ended up costing $27,575. Credit cards became de rigueur, the indie norm.

I got lucky. Miramax had just been bought by Disney. And there was talk in the trades, "Now, Miramax is going to lose its edge." Harvey [Weinstein] has never said it, but I honestly believe Harvey was buying a movie just to shut people up; "Guess what? I'm going to pick up the scrappiest, most foul-mouthed, ugliest independent American film that there is. How about that?" *Boom!*—I got in.

Kevin Smith (left) directing 1994's *Clerks*, with actor Jeff Anderson.

The story that everyone was saying was, "He made a movie in a fucking convenience store for pennies with his friends. And he's going back to work there on Monday." People thought that that was very funny. But I really had to go back to work on Monday. Sundance was January 1994. There was a lot of travel for film festivals. I kept my job at Quick Stop and RST until August, but I was giving more interviews at the store than actually working, so I quit.

The Second Clerk Generation

"Any self-respecting, wannabe filmmaker had to take that path."

Alex Ross Perry: The film culture at the time was that you could just jump right in. If I saw *Clerks*, I could then read some interview where Kevin Smith says he was inspired by Jarmusch. And I could rent *Stranger than Paradise* (1984), and within a week I can have watched seven other Jarmusch movies. Twenty years earlier, it wouldn't have been so easy to see every movie a director had made in the span of six days, unless there was a retrospective happening. There was only so much stuff that would be appealing in the late nineties, early two-thousands, to guys like me and Joe [Swanberg]. And the benefit being that when you have access to a place that really curates itself, you can then get a lot deeper very quickly.

Joe Swanberg: I was born in 1981. In high school, when I watched *Sex, Lies, and Videotape*, it seemed like the most achievable thing in the world. It was just a bunch of people having conversations. Now, when I watch that movie, I think, "Good God, how did you do that when you were twenty-four years old?" But it wasn't daunting at the time. It was totally inspiring. I thought, "Good, here is the path. And it makes total sense to me."

Alex Ross Perry: It probably started in '94 with Kevin Smith and Tarantino—*Clerks* and then *Pulp Fiction*. That was a turning point where very culturally relevant films were being talked about by the creator in the same breath as their experience working in a video store.

Joe Swanberg: In Pierson's book, he talks to Kevin Smith throughout. And there was Tarantino and Roger Avary [director/screenwriter who also worked at Video Archives]. It seemed like the most logical thing to do. It was like, "Okay, I am fifteen years old, there are not a lot of jobs I can get anyway. I could work in fast food, maybe I could work in a movie theater. Or I could go do what all those other guys did and I can try to work in a video store."

John Pierson: I say early on that that book is meant to make you feel like you can do it too, which is important. But the other thing I really wanted to convey as much was that for the earlier wave of filmmakers, like Jarmusch and the Coens, they were inspired by filmmakers from all over the world even though they were working with meager resources. They were loving great things that other directors had done. They were reaching up. But with *Clerks*, people looked around and said, "Fuck, I could do that." Not, "Oh, that's so great." It was more, "Fuck him. I can do that." It's important to feel both things. Wow, I can really do this, but also I want to do something great.

Alex Ross Perry: I would read every interview with them. I went to Kevin Smith Q&As. I'm sure that my appreciation of them and their personalities showed me an alternative path to discovering how to create cinema. If Tarantino mentions thirty movies in an interview, I could probably get twenty of them. If people say *Reservoir Dogs* is a lot like *City on Fire*, I can go get that. And if you're like, "This movie's a lot like these Jean-Pierre Melville French crime movies," I'm like, "I can go get that, I can go see what those are all about." That's something that a filmmaker like Joe, who's around my age, could do. I was right at a time when it couldn't have been easier, and I think that that is true of a lot of filmmakers in our generation.

Joe Swanberg on the set of 2015's *Digging for Fire*.

Joe Swanberg: I worked at Hollywood Video in Naperville, Illinois, the suburbs of Chicago. There were a few indie video stores where I would rent from, but the only job I could get was at a corporate video store. The independent video stores weren't hiring. They were all family businesses. I basically turned in my application the day I turned sixteen. My friend Bob got a job there first. And then I got a job, and then three of our friends did. It became our little movie club.

Alex Ross Perry: I worked in a Sun Coast Video when I was in high school. It was in a mall. Sun Coast only sells; they don't rent. I wouldn't say it was an inspirational place, creatively, but it was fun to go hang out for eight hours, put on whatever PG movies we were allowed to watch, and just talk with a bunch of nerds who worked there.

It wasn't until I worked at Kim's, which overlaps largely with my time at film school, that the personalities I was exposed to inspired me. The bold-faced clientele there was a very inspirational group of people. I always wanted to be the kind of guy who would come into a place like that, and who might excite the clerks the way people got excited when Simon Pegg or Eli Roth came in to Kim's. Eli Roth signed a poster, like, "This was my real film school." It was always fun to see what movies Rob Zombie would buy. I saw Jarmusch in there all the time. It was important for them to make this fabled pilgrimage to Kim's Video. And if they're out-of-town people, they're not going to rent—they'll just buy a bunch of stuff. Michel Gondry came in a lot. It was fun, as a film student, to see that. It's like seeing a hero of yours doing something that you respect; it makes you feel like you're on the right track.

Joe Swanberg: Alex and I are both part of the Tarantino tradition of video clerks who became filmmakers. We both grew up thinking that that was the path you took. When I was in high school, I thought that any self-respecting, wannabe filmmaker had to take that path.

Alex Ross Perry: It's different than the seventies generation of filmmakers. You never accidentally find out that Scorsese and De Palma went to a lot of art-house movies, but it's like, "Oh, it turns out that this person lived in video stores." It's a little more instructive. I was in the stores when they were all closing, and there was already a video store generation of filmmakers before me. If now, in 2014, I'm part of it, I'm as close to the end of it as anyone could be, which is just representative of the way things have shook down.

Kevin Smith: It's weird to think that because of our flicks, a lot of people started to work at video stores hoping to get into the movie business. But I guess the

world corrected that. Good luck finding a video store
at this point.

Three Nails in the Coffin: Blockbuster, DVD, and the Internet

"I guess it's because we're a disposable culture."

In 1985, the first Blockbuster video store opened in Dallas, Texas. By 2004, there were more than nine thousand Blockbuster stores across the country. In 1997, the DVD was introduced. By 2003, DVD rentals were outperforming VHS tapes. These two developments marked major evolutions in home viewing, and they also hastened the end of video store culture. Blockbuster went bankrupt in

2010, and effectively closed its last stores in 2013. After a peak of 1.2 billion sales in 2004, DVD sales have declined precipitously, by more than thirty percent in the following decade.

Alex Ross Perry: There were two Blockbusters equidistant from my house. And they're on TV saying, "Come to Blockbuster," and me being a seven-year-old, I'd be like, "I want to go there." I recall, on several consecutive birthdays, renting *Godzilla* movies and the *Jaws* sequels. The Blockbusters were totally good. For my seven- and eight-year-old brain, they were quite sufficient.

Ira Deutchman: Little by little, Blockbuster, and then there was another chain called Hollywood Video, they started taking over the business from the mom-and-pop stores. That's when they started using their clout to try to get rid of the wholesalers and actually deal directly with the studios.

Alex Ross Perry outside of his local store Video Gallery in Brooklyn.

Larry Estes: What normally would happen is people would say, "We want *Rambo*." "Jeez, I'm sorry but we had four copies of it but they're already gone." Those stores were quickly devoured by Blockbuster. Late eighties, they had the idea to guarantee that you would get the movie you want. They'd have seventy of them instead of four. They started eating the mom-and-pops alive. People didn't want to see everything, they just wanted to see what they wanted to see, which gave Blockbuster the "in" to take over the business.

Ira Deutchman: Blockbuster put an enormous

amount of pressure on the studios to drop their inter-mediaries and to do business directly. They also did not want to pay those prices, one hundred-and-something dollars per tape. Their business model was that they would have the biggest hits and they would be never out of stock.

Doug Liman: I was the person who rented whichever movie there was the most of on the shelves. That must be the one I should see. We are herd animals when it comes to our moviegoing pref-erences. So, if there are forty copies of *Swingers*, it must be a really good, fun movie. Otherwise, the store wouldn't have so many. That was a shorthand back then. When you went to the video store and you saw a wall of one movie, that meant that it was a big movie. And if you saw one or two copies, it was a fringe art film.

Kevin Smith: It was sad when Blockbuster came in and started killing the mom-and-pop stores. RST eventually stopped renting videos because Block-buster came in literally across the highway. So sud-denly there was a place where there was a wall of new releases to pick from. But smart people kept hanging out at RST because it was such a hole in the wall.

Alex Ross Perry: In a corporate-model store like Blockbuster, new releases took up, in terms of shelf space and in terms of dollars, seventy to ninety percent. That's why the entire circumference of the store would be new releases; whereas, when you went to a place like Kim's, there were new releases, but it was no more than twenty percent of the shelf space in the entire store, if that. A corporate store was mandated to have about ten thousand movies.

Ira Deutchman: If Blockbuster wanted to buy a hundred copies for each store, if it was some big Hollywood blockbuster, there was no way in the world that they were going to pay the hundred-and-something dollars per unit. They started haggling with the studios in trying to get the prices down. The studios started making deals with Blockbuster. Instead of Blockbuster paying that flat fee, they were finally going to share in the actual revenue of the rentals. It started to evolve in that direction where they would maybe buy a certain number of copies, but then incrementally above and beyond those copies, there would be a revenue share of some kind. Then it evolved eventually to being almost totally revenue share. I think that the studios could trust the numbers more from a big company like Blockbuster, which was completely computerized, than mom-

and-pop stores, who were still, by the way, required to buy their individual copies at a hundred and twenty-five dollars apiece. Only Blockbuster was able to get deals.

Kevin Smith: But what was the crime there? They were just providing movies for people to watch. I was never that shitty about Blockbuster because it was like, "Hey, man, worst-case scenario, I can probably go to Blockbuster and find what I am looking for." It was even more sad, ironically, when Blockbuster dropped a decade later. I didn't see that coming. *Clerks* became an historical document. "In olden times, people would walk into the store…" As much as it should have been, "I'm pissing on the ashes of these corporate tyrants," it just was like, "Oh, my god, it's all ending." Everything we'd known. This magical event of going to the video store from my childhood, that way of life was going to go away.

Nicole Holofcener: Your bar just gets lower and lower. I was just at a Barnes and Noble, and I was so happy it was still there. Barnes and Noble had been the enemy. And so was Blockbuster. I really miss cruising the aisles and choosing movies that way.

Ira Deutchman: That change to revenue share was

a major change in the business model that became available to the Blockbusters and chains, but not to the mom-and-pop stores. So that was a nail in the coffin of the traditional model. The DVD business becoming a sell-through business was another nail in the coffin in the rental business. The original DVD players were the fastest-adopted new technology in the history of modern electronics. There were more DVD players sold in a shorter period of time than any other invention that had ever been put on the market. That was mainly because the films were put on the market so cheaply.

Janet Pierson: I switched to DVD as soon as I could. I remember John was sort of resistant, but I was like, "This is so much better. I want this. I want this upgrade."

Ira Deutchman: It was Warren Lieberfarb who was running Warner Home Video, who released a slew of Warner Brothers titles. And released them right from the get-go at sell-through prices without even thinking about the rental market. That began the explosion of the DVD market. There were a lot of people in the studio system who were really upset at Warner's for doing that, because they thought that they had sold it short. In reality, it's the reason why it became such a huge market so quickly. That became yet another business model.

Kevin Smith: In the LaserDisc commentary for *Chasing Amy* (1997), I said, "Fuck DVD," because it was coming and about to change everything.

Ira Deutchman: The most recent wrinkle on all of this is that now that we're heading into a world where people are used to being able to stream things whenever, and wherever they want, there's no real feeling of people wanting to own anything. It means that by creating a marketplace built around sell-through on DVD, it almost guaranteed that the DVD market was going to collapse. Which is exactly what's happened. The only movies that people buy anymore are things that are truly collectibles.

Darren Aronofsky: It's amazing how that has all completely disappeared. I have all of those DVDs in binders. I spent a lot of time alphabetizing them. I don't go to them anymore because I can pretty much get everything through streaming. Although, sometimes, I have to go down to the basement to get something.

Greg Mottola: It was very depressing to me when the DVD market dried up. I don't understand why people are really okay with everything being digital. I understand the convenience. I guess it's because we're a disposable culture. But to me, DVDs don't cost that much money. I'd rather just own it. But I'm a film guy.

Kevin Smith: Whenever you hear, "way of life," it sounds vaguely like old white men saying, "I wish it was the fifties again." But it really was the first time in my life where I said, "My God, my way of life is going away."

Ira Deutchman: The delivery systems keep changing, but the reality is that the business models keep pretty constant because there are only a limited number of business models for content. You have the video-on-demand (VOD) model, where you actually are buying the viewing of the particular film, and ironically VOD includes theatrical. VOD is delivered by different pipes. The old video rental model was a crude version of the VOD model. People were paying for a rental and then they had to return it. And then you have the subscription model, which includes everything from Netflix to HBO; delivering via different pipes, but it's pretty much the same thing. And there's the free model, which is typically paired with advertising, like YouTube or network television. And then there is the buy-to-own collector model, which is getting killed to some extent because people don't seem that interested in it. These things tend to cycle, so maybe with a change in the technology there might be a disruption for a period of time, but then it settles back into being one of those four models again.

Wake Up Streaming

"That's the most depressing thing I've ever heard in my life."

Quentin Tarantino: I am not excited about streaming at all. I like something hard and tangible in my hand. And I can't watch a movie on a laptop. I don't use Netflix at all. I don't have any sort of delivery system. I have the videos from Video Archives. They went out of business, and I bought their inventory. Probably close to eight thousand tapes and DVDs.

Kevin Smith: That's kind of genius. He's such a sentimental dude.

Quentin Tarantino: I have a bunch of DVDs and a

bunch of videos, and I still tape movies off of television on video so I can keep my collection going.

Allison Anders: Now, it's boring to go online. "All right, I picked that out and you picked this out." It's boring.

David O. Russell: The other night, I'm trying to plan my evening's activities. I want to unwind and watch a classic. My wife says, "Not looking good." I come into the bedroom and I say, "What about this one? What about this one?" She checks, and goes, "Look." I go, "Jesus, but there's mountains of garbage." I'll read you a list: *The Only Game in Town*, George Stevens's last film after *Giant*, with Warren Beatty and Elizabeth Taylor. You can't get it on any of these venues. *Back Street* with Susan Hayward; *Thrill of Romance* with Van Johnson and Esther Williams; *Another Part of the Forest*, which is a prequel to *The Little Foxes*; *From the Terrace* with Paul Newman; *A Summer Place*, which is a classic film; *The Revolt of Mamie Stover*. There's a lot of stuff going on with the licensing and the deals where they no longer have certain movies. It used to be that Amazon had everything, but Amazon changed their deal. And I'll say it to the guy I know who owns Netflix: it's a bunch of dreck.

J.C. Chandor: They are figuring it all out slowly. In the next four or five years, whether it be from Amazon or Apple, you'll be able to get anything you want with the click of a mouse.

Alex Ross Perry: I started trying to get into downloading movies, and I just never watched any of them.

Doug Liman: It's awfully convenient to click on something on your laptop and get it. I remain excited for the future.

Tim Blake Nelson: I love the streaming feature. I love that I can sit in my house and for four bucks I can watch *The Treasure of the Sierra Madre* and I don't have to deal with commercials. And I have control of the experience. I love Netflix and Apple TV. Eventually, I think everything will be on there.

Morgan Spurlock: Now I can have access to all of them, whether it be on Netflix, or on my television. Now, the library that used to be down in that trailer at the end of my street when I was a kid is in my house, which is even more amazing.

Richard Gladstein: I showed my kids *To Kill a Mockingbird*. I pushed a button on my TV, and that's like a video store, as far as I'm concerned. You can get what you want. You just don't have to go to a store. You just have to press a button.

Greg Mottola: Netflix, in a sense, has recreated part of the store experience. I'll spend forty-five minutes or an hour scrolling through box art until I find something. It drives my wife crazy.

Janet Pierson: Most people don't have the boxes anymore, but what they have are "likes." And they have this community of Twitter followers, and they have conversations. So there's still fandom, and there are gatherings in different ways.

John Pierson: It's great to think that we're going to reach a time when we can watch anything we need to watch. But as someone who has been involved in films and as a rights holder and one who believes in protecting those rights, I am torn. I wish more things were more available. And it feels like we're in a moment when we are switching away from, "The sky's the limit."

Greg Mottola: I am an owner. Every movie that is really important to me, I either own it on VHS or DVD or LaserDisc. I like to reference that stuff.

Kevin Smith: You can't get a kid today to relate to that. My kid's grown up watching Blu-ray and DVDs, and now she's deep in the stream and in the clouds. Try to communicate to someone like that, "There was a time when you couldn't watch anything whenever you wanted." Of course, you can't watch *Guardians of the Galaxy* until they let you, but I'm talking back then it was anything. You couldn't watch *Star Wars*. People look at you like you're crazy.

Janet Pierson: I used to have a miserably weird, bad reaction to video stores. Too many boxes of cereal; I didn't know which one I wanted. If you look at Netflix, the lineup, that's working for me so much better than video stores did.

Joe Swanberg: I saw a movie, *The Telephone Book* from 1971, the other day. This weirdo sex movie popped up on Netflix. I was like, "Okay, cool. They're licensing some cool stuff that is off of my radar." When I was fourteen, I wanted to be a filmmaker, and I started reading *Filmmaker Magazine* and I'd read about indie films I'd never see, not even at the video store. These days, you can see them on VOD. If I was fourteen right now, still in the suburbs of Chicago, I could be really up-to-date with the independent film scene as much as anyone in L.A. or NYC. That's exciting. The access is getting better.

Darren Aronofsky: I'm a newcomer to Netflix. I can't wait for a seminal, "Kim's Streaming" type of experience where you can get any title you want. There seems like someone should get on it. There are so many good films. And there are too many that are hard to get. Netflix is limited that way. I like their original programming, but I can't say I use it for much else. Although, I did hear about a Gael García Bernal film, *Even the Rain* (2010). It's a film he made in Bolivia. It's fantastic—and you can watch it on Netflix. The experience was very similar to how I would stumble on a film on videotape. It's a small, beautiful foreign film. And I streamed it.

Joe Swanberg: The blogs are never going to be a video store replacement. But a Fandor or equivalent website can be like that well-cultivated college-town video store, where you can't find an Adam Sandler movie but you can find every Werner Herzog film. That kind of curation. Fandor's whole vibe is not that they are going to have every movie that's available. They're going to have thirty movies that are going to be available to you now, and all of them are going to be good.

Ira Deutchman: The online marketplace has not matured enough to take the place of the revenues that are disappearing on the DVD side. There's a sense that maybe eventually it will. Of course, it's a much more fragmented market, which is probably pretty scary to the studios because they're highly dependent on the blockbuster mentality, perhaps more than ever. Where they want to put something out on the marketplace and know they're going to be able to sell millions and millions of copies. They built a business model based around the idea that they only manufacture product that's capable of selling millions and millions of copies. Meanwhile, the actual online marketplace is fragmenting into a million different pieces.

That whole business model in the eighties, where you could essentially get an independent film financed by virtue of having a certain amount of guaranteed home video units that it was going to sell, which matured even further in the DVD era, simply doesn't exist anymore. There are still people who try. But it would be stretching the truth. Because nobody has any numbers to back up how much business these things could potentially do on all of the various platforms that are out there now.

Greg Mottola: I don't know where things will end up with streaming revenue. It seems like a lot of companies are making a lot of money, but it's not ending up in the pockets of artists very much.

John Sayles: The numbers aren't there for that dream of someone downloading your movie and paying you for that movie. The money is not coming back.

Joe Swanberg: Home video sales used to be a significant piece of the puzzle. But I feel very lucky about the time when I was born. It has been easier to make movies than it has ever been. I got out of film school when you could make a feature film for two thousand dollars. It was such a different universe.

Doug Liman: I think it's a pretty good time to be a new filmmaker. They don't even need distribution. They can put it out on the web themselves. There are so many opportunities. They can make a film for a lot less money than it cost us to make *Swingers*. When I made *Swingers*, without a Miramax or a Buena Vista, no one could see the movie. It wouldn't see the light of day.

Kevin Smith: You'd think I'm like, "Fuck streaming. Because in our day . . ." But I'm a filmmaker who is happy to watch a film on an iPhone. I just want to get it in me. I'm a movie lover at heart, so the quickest, easiest way you can get it to me is A-okay in my book. It doesn't have to be on an IMAX screen. That's great, sometimes. But I need it in me. I just need the movie in me. Any way that that can be administered, even if it's on a tiny iPhone screen. I like streaming.

John Sayles: It used to be that you could go to a theater and the print that was playing was actually three different prints spliced together, and one bulb and one projector was off, and each reel would be darker or lighter or redder. And it wasn't what the cinematographer wanted it to look like. The nice thing about digital is, when you sign off on the look of a picture, that's it.

J.C. Chandor: I used to come into the city, to the art-houses, to watch movies in theaters that probably are technologically inferior to what most decent home theaters are now.

Darren Aronofsky: Most people are going to watch my films on an iPhone. We talk about that. When we did a sound mix, we did an iPad or iPhone mix for *Noah*, so that hopefully it would be in stereo. "Look," I said, "there's a real audience there, and you have to be conscious of that. You can't control it."

Quentin Tarantino: That's the most depressing thing I've ever heard in my life.

Darren Aronofsky: It's probably why I have moved to 1.85 [aspect ratio] in my framing on films. [Aronofsky went from 1.85 for *The Fountain* to 2.35 for *The Wrestler* and *Black Swan*, and back to 1.85 for *Noah.*] It's closer to what people are actually going to see on a hand-held device. It's the reality. I do a lot of sound work. That's the biggest loss. Sound is a big part of filmmaking, and even with your Beats headphones, you're missing the whole surround-sound feeling. In the end, I am a storyteller, and I want my story to be watched and listened to in any possible form. I can't be snobbish about it. I would like people to see it in the theater, but I recognize that people see them in all sorts of ways and I try to make that experience as good as I can.

What's Lost

"When did the world start getting so fat? Probably when they stopped walking to the video store."

Alex Ross Perry: [On the way to being interviewed near his home in Brooklyn, Perry walked by his local video store, Video Gallery, which announced the week before that it would be closing.] It's just a bummer, because for me, that experience has continued uninterrupted until now. From going to Blockbuster when I was five or six, there's never been a time in my life when I couldn't say, "I'm going to go wander around the video store." I went to Video Gallery two or three times a week. Now, that experience is gone from my life. I lived a hundred feet away from the last remaining option. There is no other option for me now.

Quentin Tarantino: I think it's really, really sad. This next generation isn't going to know what it's missing. The mom-and-pop video stores around L.A. and New York have closed. But it has taken longer to close around America. When I was doing *Django* (2012), I went on a location scout in Tennessee. They had just closed the stores. But the signs were still there. "R & J Video." "Bob's Video." "Wong's Video." The blood on the wound was still fresh. It made me sad. Something's lost: that can't be denied.

J.C. Chandor: It all seems so quaint now.

Nicole Holofcener: My kids think we're talking about the horse and buggy.

James Franco: We are losing a place where people can go and meet face-to-face and know that there is some sort of central meeting place for people who love film. As a creative person, I love to find the communities that appreciate the things I love. That's where I do my best work. If I am making the work for those kinds of people, people who are knowledgeable about the things I'm doing, then I feel like I am using the medium for everything that it can be. The Internet is nice because it turns that community into a wider thing where I could meet someone who loves *Aguirre* and, "Okay, let's have a Herzog festival." It can build communities. But I liked knowing that there was a center where you could go.

Joe Swanberg: One of the biggest achievements I ever felt as a filmmaker was when Cinefile Video in Los Angeles made a section for my movies in their "Directors" section. You can't find my stuff in the comedy or drama section—you have to go to the Joe Swanberg section. Kids won't even know what that means. My son won't know what it means that there was a section where six of my movies were on a shelf with my nameplate underneath it. For me, it was like, "Holy shit. I am a filmmaker."

Nicole Holofcener: It was really important to me. I really wanted to get my own shelf. The Vidiots store, they gave me a shelf even though I had five movies instead of six. It's funny, the small gift that makes you feel like you've arrived. Seeing my name next to Werner Herzog, I was like, "This is really cool."

Darren Aronofsky: I remember the day when I walked in to Kim's and I saw that I got a section. That was a big moment. They put your name on a piece of masking tape. I was under Wes Anderson, and I remember taking a photo and sending it to him. It was a rite of passage.

David O. Russell: It was a big deal for me when I got my director's shelf at Vidiots.

Allison Anders: There was nothing more exciting than when you saw you had a shelf. "Oh, my God, my work as a director is valued in this way."

Joe Swanberg: For me, it was the about breadth and width. The Internet has made everything a straight line. You have something you are interested in, you Google it, you go right there. The video store was walking down the aisle and looking at shelves and turning over a hundred and fifty different boxes and stumbling upon stuff you didn't know existed. A big part was about discovery. That's what's gone away in my life. I still go to bookstores. But I haven't gone to a video store and rented a movie in eight or nine years.

Los Angeles's Vidiots store found new life after turning non-profit. Credit: Lore Dach

Kevin Smith: It's just gratification, now. The anticipation is gone. As a customer, it was anticipation and—*if* it was there—gratification. And if it's not, "Fuck!" And you were forced to get something else, and suddenly, your taste grew. You were like, "Fuck, the movie I wanted wasn't there so I wound up getting this, but this movie was fucking amazing, man." You don't get that with streaming. What I want to see, I'll see it when I want it.

Alex Ross Perry: I'm sure there's a vast loss, but I'm sure that if I were fifteen now, my viewing habits would be different. If I'm fifteen in 2014, I'd probably have a hard drive with twenty thousand titles, because if I want to get into Cronenberg, forty-five minutes later, I have twenty-seven movies to watch.

Kevin Smith: We're a nation of spoiled babies at this

point. I think it's awesome. I'm one of those spoiled babies. Look, we're all headed toward *Wall-E*. We're going to be big, fat fucking versions of ourselves, or bigger and fatter in my case, floating on deck chairs drinking cupcakes out of shake straws and watching programming. That's A-okay with me. When did the world start getting so fat? Probably when they stopped walking to the video store.

Alex Ross Perry: I don't know if the way that I appreciated videos is simply impossible in the same way as no one can appreciate sitting on the porch like they used to, listening to the radio, anymore. I don't know if it's that vast. I would imagine that it's just impossible to, in the span of ten years, completely breed out of people the simple appreciation of consuming as much stuff as you can possibly get your hands on because you have nothing else to do. Not to sound like an old fogey, but there was a joy about the anticipation of having to wait until the weekend to even go browse the videos, much less watch them. And there was the joy of successfully lobbying for transportation to a store, and a joy of being there for however long you're allowed to be. That certainly cannot exist anymore. I had to wait until Friday nights to go and get my viewing haul for the weekend. Anyone now could be downloading three hundred movies between Monday and Friday.

Joe Swanberg: It's too early in the game to talk about the generation of filmmakers that grew up on Netflix. We don't know who they are yet. My guess is that we are going to be amazed by them, and also we'll be bitching about the same things. Some stupid movie that's really popular on Netflix now will be getting remade and we'll be like, "That wasn't even good the first time." But they saw it when they were twelve and loved it.

Alex Ross Perry: I'm sure in fifteen years there'll be some other filmmaker talking about all the specific ways that downloading torrents of movies shaped his definition of cinema, and it will make as little sense to me as this would to somebody else.

Joe Swanberg: It's funny to remember someone would be like, "Hey, do you want to do this?" And I'd be like, "No, I can't, I have to finish watching this movie and get to the video store before seven o'clock." It's funny to think how differently we spent our time then.

Darren Aronofsky: There was always that time you'd go to a video store, and there was so much selection, and you would stand around and debate. "Oh, I've seen that." "Oh, that's bad." You just had conversation after conversation. But it's not something I am necessarily going to miss.

Joe Swanberg: It is easy to romanticize the best video stores I ever went to. But I'd say that the best ones, like Facets, are still in business. Now, they are a whole different thing. They are catering to a different clientele. I don't know that we are missing a ton with the loss of the average mom-and-pop store. I'm guilty of being nostalgic, and I'll probably tell my kids, "Boy, it was cool when you could just go in there." But also, you know, late fees and having to rewind. There was a lot of bullshit that went along with it that I won't miss at all.

Quentin Tarantino: I don't remember that ever being a problem. And the late fees were usually nothing. Usually, clerks knocked it off to forty cents on the dollar. That's a problem? The late fees? No, the idea of going to the video store has somehow become passé. And I don't understand it. I guess people want to become shut-ins.

Joe Swanberg: VHS was never the ideal screening format to watch a movie. We are already talking about a bastardized version of a work of art, right? It's like a third generation of a painting: a printed poster of a photograph of the Mona Lisa. If we were talking about Warner Bros. burning their archives or something, I'd say, "Wait a minute, guys, we should think this over." We are talking about brick-and-mortar stores so that you could have access to this stuff. But it was not ideal—often pan-and-scanned, or bad versions of these movies. Now that we have iTunes and Netflix and HD versions of that stuff, the only thing we are losing is the browsing and interfacing with a person.

Alex Ross Perry: Working in a great place like Kim's, I was inspired by the people, which is really the valuable part of video store culture; you're likely to surround yourself with people who will inspire you—more so than the movies themselves. That's definitely something that no one's going to get on a torrent, and no one's going to get in any other way, because you can be a kid who downloads ten thousand movies and watches all of them. But that won't make you a good filmmaker, nor will it teach you how to make movies. Working with three other people who also want to make movies will do more for you than any number of movies you can consume on your own.

Doug Liman: I grew up with my experiences being curated, and I do think we still like to have our experiences curated. You can have the best of both worlds if you can choose your curator. Back when I was coming up in this business, you couldn't choose your curator. It was whatever video store was closest to you. I liken it to what was happening in the news way back when everyone listened to Walter Cronkite and that was the truth. Your experience in television news was very curated. Your moviegoing experience was curated when you would go to the video store. You didn't think, "How did those movies end up on the shelves?" I didn't until I experienced that *Swingers* weekend that the studios were hosting. You lose a little. But it can't be bad to democratize people's moviegoing experience.

Richard Gladstein: One of my last experiences at a video store, I went to the one on Sunset Boulevard near Sunset Plaza. I was in line. And there was a guy in front of me, and I glanced over his shoulder and I saw that he was buying five copies of the same movie. I looked closer, and on the jacket was a guy who looked like Johnny Depp, and the movie was *Edward Penishands*. It was the porn version of *Edward Scissorhands*. When I got to the counter, I asked the guy, "Can I get a copy of that?" He said, "He just bought the last copies. Do you know who that was? It was Tim Burton." I was like, "Really?" This pimply kid was dead serious. That ain't happening if you stay home and stream movies.

David O. Russell: To this day, I love going to video stores. It's a destination. I don't like that everything's in your house. It's all on your computer. It's very isolating.

Luc Besson: What they should maybe do is have an Amazon club or Netflix club like Starbucks, where you can take a drink. It would be a new kind of video club where you can get a coffee and you have a little cabin to see a movie. And people can talk. And directors can go to speak.

Larry Estes: You need to have a certain amount of knowledge of what has become before, but even a store with Scarecrow's title depth and the manic insistence on quality and availability is not getting enough people, because of Internet delivery. And as much as the business tries to stop piracy, it is too fast-moving. File sharing: That's the main reason movies can't sell to the depth that they used to, because people don't pay for them. It is becoming people who just like the environment of going into a store with thousands of DVDs and director sections. But it's like *Dawn of the Dead*. Zombies walking around this place, because they like the way it feels. If only a few places in the world still have libraries like that, they need to be treated like museums and they need to get more funding. There's a hopeful, guarded optimism that someone will stand up and wave that flag, but it's more and more financially difficult. It really is following the music business.

Quentin Tarantino: It's a cultural thing that has been lost. And nothing worthwhile has taken its place. To tell you the truth, I don't know why it was lost. Is it just leaving the house? People don't want to leave the house any more? Is that it? I'm asking you.

Kevin Smith: He's obviously very special. That's why we get what we get out of him. Why doesn't anyone want to go to the video store? Of course, they don't want to. It's one less thing for them to do in the world when everyone is anxious to save time and create more time to do stuff that they need more time to create time from.

Quentin Tarantino: Progress is not leaving the house? That's progress? I like eating at home, but I like eating in a restaurant, too, even though I have a kitchen at home.

Kevin Smith: The trip to the video store is pretty much eliminated, and people like it that way. In the rush forward, the video store got left behind. It's like that scene in *Almost Famous* when they walk away from the bus and head toward the plane. Sometimes we go so fucking fast, we don't see the endings of things that were vastly important to us. But I slowed down to see the end of the video store, because I said, "There goes my whole way of life. Everything I knew is gone." It's like watching Krypton explode from earth. That's it. My home is gone. It'll never happen again.

Appendix: "Passing of a Video Store and a Downtown Aesthetic"

The New York Times, July 24th, 2014

When Kim's Video & Music announced that this summer it would be closing its last store, on First Avenue in the East Village, written tributes ranged from the resigned to the exultant. "Kim's was this portal into New York City I never came back from," Eddie Huang, the restaurateur, author and television personality, wrote in a blog post. "Everything in my life, I can somehow attribute to finding Kim's."

Of course, the jig had been up since Kim's flagship store, on St. Marks Place, shuttered in 2009. The owner, Yongman Kim, consolidated what had grown to a four-store empire into one, and he shipped his 55,000-film collection to Sicily, where there was a fairy-tale promise that the films would find new life.

Pressed by higher rents, Mr. Kim said, he plans to close the First Avenue store at the end of next month, 27 years after he opened the first one, on Avenue A, in 1987. But this is more than a story of rising rents and the disruption wrought by digital streaming. It's the tale of a downtown culture now largely lost, one in which clerks and creative types mingled, influencing one another and the scene as well.

"Kim's was where we went to get our gold," said the filmmaker and New York University film professor Alexandre Rockwell ("In the Soup") "They had porn, B movies and highbrow art films. Kim's made film funky and accessible to people who were hanging out and getting high and bussing tables who stumbled in."

The cultural stamp that Kim's left on the city wasn't entirely of its own creation. "When the Kim's brand was being built, that esoteric sense of low cinema was completely in line with the East Village," said the director Alex Ross Perry ("The Color Wheel"). "Nobody who had a business in that part of town invented it, but if you wanted to be relevant, I am sure it was clear who your customers were going to be."

The neighborhood had already spawned the no wave scene, encompassing punk music and movies. There were the anti-establishment fringe films of Scott B and Beth B and later the European-inspired work of Jim Jarmusch and others who took in movies at Anthology Film Archives and the Millennium Film Workshop, a postproduction house that also held screenings.

And they embraced Kim's as their own.

"The moment Kim's opened, it supplanted everything else in the area," said the musician and writer Richard Hell. "It was so much better curated."

Mr. Hell, 64, came of age nearby, in a Lower East Side of the 1970s, where "there was no relief from the poverty and filth."

"It was all so ruined that kids like me could afford to live there," he added. "So you had a society that was stimulating, and you shared a lot of purpose."

For Aaron Bondaroff, a 37-year-old downtown artist and store owner who has run galleries and recently started Know Wave, a live online radio show, "If you were looking for inspiration, Kim's was a great place to go, whether you were designing or making music or a zine."

It was part of Mr. Bondaroff's downtown route, as

he put it. For a time, you could go treasure hunting at the Strand for books, the vintage hot spot Antique Boutique for clothes, and Kim's for videos. Kim's also had a deep and eclectic music collection, but there were closer rivals for that, like Tower Records, Bleecker Bob's and Other Music.

The act of browsing "was an incredibly valuable and fun experience," Mr. Perry said. "That is essentially dead, especially in terms of home video purchase."

As a film student at New York University, Mr. Perry said, he fed his "insatiable appetite for consuming cinema" at Kim's and eventually went to work there as a clerk for three years, one of several employees who went on to different warrens of the culture. Workers at one time or another included the filmmaker Robert Greene (the coming "Actress"), Albert Hammond Jr. of the Strokes and the cartoonist Leslie Stein (the comic series Eye of the Majestic Creature).

In addition to the diaspora of former clerks, there are the countless customers who were affected in ways big or small. "I remember the day I walked in and saw that I got a section," the director Darren Aronofsky ("Noah") said. "That was a big moment."

Mr. Huang said, "You'll see Kim's in my food and my work." Kim's clerks had a reputation for arrogance, but Mr. Huang said he would emulate their rough edge at his restaurant Baohaus, when it was on Rivington Street. (Now it's on 14th Street.) Customers would ask, " 'Yo, you got cha siu bao?' ," referring to Cantonese pork buns. " 'No, I don't have cha siu bao,' " he would tell them. " 'You're going to eat *this*, and you are going to learn something today.' "

As for Mr. Kim, sitting behind a drab desk in his basement office in the First Avenue store, he said that he was "happy to have been involved in this," but that he was feeling defeated.

"I am the loser," he said. "Netflix is the winner."

Mr. Kim emigrated from South Korea to the Lower East Side in 1979, and studied at the School of Visual Arts. When his Avenue A dry cleaning business was up and running in 1986, he dedicated a corner to movie rentals. The first Kim's Video arrived year later.

"My personal style was more French and early Russian realism," he said. "I still believe the silent is the real form of film. Because too much dialogue builds barriers between people and nations."

A taste shaped by his immigrant experience dovetailed well with his business sense: He began his library by soliciting thousands of free titles from the Bulgarian and Czechoslovakian cultural consulates.

And Kim's also stocked relatively cheap B movies

that fit his aesthetic. "The directors and set designers are using their own hands," he said. "It's real. A Hollywood set is so fake."

But as rents rose and streaming services squeezed his business, Mr. Kim scrambled for years to develop an online business that eventually faltered.

When he couldn't get a nearby institution to accept his library on his terms, he sent it to Salemi, Italy, at the urging of some artists and politicians who supported a plan to revitalize the town as a center of arts tourism. Mr. Kim visited there two years ago. The situation was "a total mess," he said. "Sadly, I don't know what's going on."

Mr. Kim is taking business classes and plans to return with the Kim's brand in some way. He's also thinking of moving back to the Lower East Side from New Jersey, where he now lives.

He'd be returning to a different downtown.

"Manhattan in the 21st century is this Disneyland for the superrich," Mr. Hell said, even though he cautioned against romanticizing the past. "New York in the '70s was more like the reality of human existence. And you need to know what the world is really like to make good art."

Mr. Bondaroff suggested younger generations would find cultural inspiration where it can. "It's a different struggle now," he said. "The struggle is against corporate America opening stores on Avenue B. Anyway, where does a creative person go? Europe? Red Hook? It's up to you how creative you are."

Acknowledgements

Thanks first to the gatekeepers—the assistants and publicists and agents—whom I pestered in order to get to the filmmakers. Cynthia Swartz, in particular, has always been a helpful hand, and she once again came through for me here.

My gratitude goes mostly to the filmmakers, and it begins with appreciation for their films that shaped me. And there are other influences, like Reid Rosefelt, publicist extraordinaire, and George Feltenstein, VP at Warner Home Video, both of whom helped shape this book. As did maestro Gary Meister.

Movies became a part of my professional life when I worked at *Premiere* magazine, so I am indebted to all who worked with me there. Thanks to Simon Brennan for bringing me over, and to the many colleagues who helped steer me, including

Leslie Van Buskirk, Rachel Clarke, Chris Cronis, Kathy Heintzelman, Howard Karren, Jason Matloff, Jim Meigs, Holly Millea, Sean Smith, Michael Solomon, Tim Swanson, Andy Webster, and that phoenix of movie reporting, Anne Thompson. My time there wouldn't have been the same without Glenn Kenny, a tour de force who could himself be the subject of an oral history. And above all, I'd like to thank Peter Herbst.

Tom Elrod, editor and founder of The Critical Press, gave me the green light and shepherded this book through, so he has more than earned his Executive Producer credit for this project. Thanks for your trust, Tom.

I want to also thank my mom, to whom I owe everything, including my first Betamax and the allowance that kept me awash in Malcolm McDowell films; and my brother, Richard, who led the way to Jim Jarmusch, the Cable Car and beyond.

And, most of all, thanks to my wife, Sandee, with whom I share a history that extends back to walking the video store aisles together. Not everyone can say that. Thanks, San, for more movie nights than I could count, and for tolerating the hours I spent writing, transcribing and interviewing for this book.

And a big hug for my movie-loving girls, Natalie and Maxine. You are, indeed, growing up in a world of streams and clouds, so it must seem silly when I get nostalgic for plastic tapes and grungy aisles. Never mind, I'm learning to let go.